FORGIVE & FORGET

God's Love Towards Mankind

Isaac O. Ajibolorunrin

Grosvenor House
Publishing Limited

All rights reserved
Copyright © Isaac O. Ajibolorunrin, 2023

The right of Isaac O. Ajibolorunrin to be identified as the author of this work has been asserted in accordance with Section 78 of the Copyright, Designs and Patents Act 1988

The book cover is copyright to Isaac O. Ajibolorunrin

This book is published by
Grosvenor House Publishing Ltd
Link House
140 The Broadway, Tolworth, Surrey, KT6 7HT.
www.grosvenorhousepublishing.co.uk

This book is sold subject to the conditions that it shall not, by way of trade or otherwise, be lent, resold, hired out or otherwise circulated without the author's or publisher's prior consent in any form of binding or cover other than that in which it is published and without a similar condition including this condition being imposed on the subsequent purchaser.

A CIP record for this book
is available from the British Library

ISBN 978-1-80381-219-9
eBook ISBN 978-1-80381-220-5

New King James Version

Scripture taken from the New King James Version®. Copyright © 1982 by Thomas Nelson. Used by permission. All rights reserved. Unless otherwise stated, all Bible passages quoted in this book are from New King James Version, (NKJV).

Amplified Bible (AMP)

Copyright © 2015 by The Lockman Foundation, La Habra, CA 90631.
All rights reserved.

The Living Bible

Life Application Bible, Verses marked TLB are taken from The Living Bible copyright © 1971. Used by permission of Tyndale House Publishers, Inc., Wheaton, Illinois 60189. All rights reserved.

DEDICATION

This book is dedicated to my son
Joshua Ayobami Ajibolorunrin,
(Josh) aka OluwaJoshua – *forever in my heart.*

FOREWORD

The author of this book has challenged and reminded us about 'The Doctrine of Forgiveness.' He has drawn examples from both the Old and New Testaments, from early church history and personal experiences. He has given us a balanced view about how to forgive and forget. Dr Ajibolorunrin has clearly stated how we can love and forgive as if we have never been hurt. I recommend this book to Christians everywhere.

Professor Clinton L. Ryan, Th.D., FRSA.
Professor of Divinity for Canada Christian College and School of Graduate Theological Studies.

Dr Isaac Ajibolorunrin is the author of this work, he has done his research on the subject of 'forgiveness'. And whenever you stand praying, if you have anything against anyone, forgive him that your Father in heaven may also forgive you your trespasses. Mark 11:25, NKJV. In this publication he emphasised in Mark 11:25, the contents of this book is the written evidence of the author that as a Christian one ought to forgive. The chapters embrace some of the most important and needed things that Christians should learn and practice and understand. His experience in Ministry has enabled him to publish this wonderful book. The principles he has written about can also be applied in a secular organisation.

Dr Isaac Ajibolorunrin has formatted each chapter into readable sections that can be easily read, discussed and studied in the Church and also for Bible students, Pastors, individuals and groups who are called by God to lead His people in His vineyard.

Dr Isaac Ajibolorunrin is passionate that as Ministers of God forgiveness is key to men and women who lead and exhort in the Church, whatever the capacity of the congregation they lead. He stressed that there is no short cut to forgiveness. He further stressed that regardless, God's expectation is that all humans will forgive their fellows. Unsurprisingly therefore, as Lewis Smedes clearly stated, *"God invented forgiveness so that He can come to terms with a world He already knew at their best would be unfair to each other and hurt each other deeply, and He began by forgiving us and goes on to invite us to forgive each other,"*[1]

And we have to learn to forgive, that is an essential element of Church growth and development, in other words we must benchmark our conduct with Christ's standard. Dr Isaac Ajibolorunrin referred to this process as a Spiritual Health Check, we must examine our character and behaviour so that we can be an example for others to emulate as highlighted in the Scripture. He has pointed out that the Church and the world community lack forgiveness therefore, suffering from a crisis of Leadership in the Ministry, marriages and even Nations rising against Nations. These are as a result of a lack of forgiveness.

Dr Isaac Ajibolorunrin is encouraging us all to forgive and forget as commanded by God. And as a Minister he has called us all to rethink and reposition ourselves for a Holy Service. Romans 12:1: "I beseech you therefore, brethren, by

---

[1] Lewis B. Smedes, *Forgive and Forget - Healing the Hurts We Don't Deserve*, New York: HarperCollins Publishers, 1966, pp. xv-xvi

the mercies of God, that you present your bodies a living sacrifice, holy, acceptable to God, *which is* your reasonable service." Ministers of the word are needed in the Church and not prosperity preachers who deceive people for their selfish gain. From my point of view he has called us all to rise up and effect change in our various Churches, homes and the workplace so that the world will be a better place for you and I. He also states that time is a healer, with time hurt or anger will subside and thereafter, you are free from all discomfort created by anger.

I believe that Jesus Christ was and is the most effective leader the world has ever known, who loved us unconditionally. It is with unreserved joy that I recommend this book to you.

Professor Isaac Ojutalayo, DMin, DD, DLitt

Head of Faculty, All Nations Bible College & School of Theological Studies, London, UK in affiliation with Canada Christian College and School of Graduate & Theological Studies, Toronto, Canada.

ENDORSEMENT

Forgive and Forget is a very timely, relevant and practical book in a world gripped with much pain, hurt and betrayal as we see the signs of the end engulf our existence. Dr Isaac Ajibolorunrin has done an exemplary job of using humanity to explain divinity, making the matter of forgiveness simple and sensible whilst complex and complicated in reality. In this book he encourages us with many biblical scriptures on this topic to ensure that we grasp that the standard God sets, sets the standard regarding forgiving and forgetting.

In his varying analogies and examples on addressing forgiving and forgetting, he seldom referred to the heart, the seat of all emotions, as a key area of contention. In my own words, I believe this book simply encourages us that the heart of the matter is the matter of the heart when considering forgiveness. In many ways, this book implores us to guard our hearts, to gauge our minds to guide our acts, in other words to guard our feelings to gauge our thinking to guide our doing.

Some scriptural references include, Philippians 4:7:, KJV: "And the peace of God, which passeth all understanding, shall keep your hearts and minds through Christ Jesus." Proverbs 4:23: "Keep your heart with all diligence, For out of it spring the issues of life." Indeed the biblical and practical examples in this book illustrates clearly that God chooses the heart above the act.

The Twelve Principles to Aid Your Journey To Freedom that Dr Isaac Ajibolorunrin states in this book are practical efforts to guide us as we all journey this path to making forgiving and forgetting a lifestyle. I am personally encouraged by this book as it confirms my conviction that forgiving even before being offended as a mindset and lifestyle helps with dealing with hurt, pain and all that ensues from it.

I implore us all to pray daily, Isaiah 11:1–4, NIV: states, "1 A shoot will come up from the stump of Jesse; from his roots a Branch will bear fruit. 2 The Spirit of the Lord will rest on him – the Spirit of wisdom and of understanding, the Spirit of counsel and of might, the Spirit of the knowledge and fear of the Lord – 3 and he will delight in the fear of the Lord. He will not judge by what he sees with his eyes, or decide by what he hears with his ears; 4 but with righteousness he will judge the needy, with justice he will give decisions for the poor of the earth. He will strike the earth with the rod of his mouth; with the breath of his lips he will slay the wicked."

This book and Isaiah 11:1-4, appeal to us as it pertains to *Forgive and Forget* that we can't act based on what we see and hear but based on righteousness and justice ably accomplished by the spirit of God being upon us and accompanied with wisdom, understanding, counsel, might, knowledge and the fear of God and in particular, a delight in the fear of God. Dr Isaac Ajibolorunrin, thank you for your diligence in authoring this simple and sensible yet substantial book, you are indeed timed before time for such a time like this by the grace and mercies of God.

What is Forgiveness and how God forgives is expressed when the Forgiver is at work and it Ignites the fire of forgiveness which helps us to be forgiveness compliant and to move forward ever like Peter whom Jesus forgave and be encouraged to be like Joseph in exercising best practice, so what are you waiting for?

Get forgiving and forgetting.

Ade Omooba MBE
Co-founder & Director
CHRISTIAN CONCERN
LONDON, UK

PREFACE

Forgiveness is a must for all Christian believers although people try to be creative, socio-tolerant, political and sophisticated about it, or shy away from it.

But the Bible is clear as stated, "Judge not, and you shall not be judged. Condemn not, and you shall not be condemned. Forgive, and you will be forgiven. Luke 6:37

It was nearing the end of summer 2019 while studying Chapter 5 in Paul's Letter to the Ephesians that a question came up about forgiveness. To be precise, it was on Sunday 22 September 2019. It was supposed to be one of the usual questions meant to be answered promptly and go on and do other things, but as it turned out, we had discussions for three Sundays in a row about forgiveness, and unfortunately we were nowhere near the end of the topic. By the third Sunday, it was agreed to organise a seminar which was scheduled for Sunday 13 October 2019. The book in your hand has been written out of the inspiration drawn from the seminar and later from the personal experiences at the time my son passed away in July 2021. This world is filled with hate, hurt, pain, betrayal, sorrow, to mention this few, and a lot of people can hide under any disguise, hence you need a book of this sort to equip you.

One of life's dilemma is facing a challenge that seems to be defying all solutions you think you know. Forgiveness is one of the issues and can be controversial. To forgive completely, forget and move on as if you were not hurt can look impossible, but in this book you will gain some helpful insights, abundant wisdom and top secrets including:

- Eight ways to help you initiate moves for forgiveness.
- Five key promises of God for you when challenged by life's issues.
- How to understand the positive effects that forgiveness provides.
- Twelve principles to aid your journey back to freedom.

I pray for a full recovery from all your pains and hurt, and trust God to let your life become exemplary. Broadly speaking, it should be noted that people are entitled to their opinion on a sensitive issue like forgiveness, but to forgive is a must. Note this statement:

> 12 And forgive us our debts, as we forgive our debtors ... 14 "For if you forgive men their trespasses, your Heavenly Father will also forgive you. 15 But if you do not forgive men their trespasses, neither will your Father forgive your trespasses. Matthew 6:12, 14–15.

ACKNOWLEDGEMENTS

I am privileged to have enjoyed the company of all those who attended some, or all the sessions where originally the subject about Forgiveness was taught during the time. I am indebted to all the members of Christ the Lord Tabernacle worldwide.

A special thanks to Pastor Ade Omooba, MBE – a man of deep insight, tremendous character and great wisdom who wrote an impartial endorsement to this book, indeed it was God who made it possible for us to meet when it happened over a decade ago.

I am particularly grateful to Professor Isaac Ojutalayo who despite the busy schedule ahead of him attended to this manuscript at a lightning speed, offered exceptional suggestions to the manuscript, wrote a comprehensive foreword to this book and worked diligently with me to ensure the deadline was not missed. I offer him my special thanks.

I must not fail to express my profound gratitude to Professor C.L. Ryan for his prompt response, special input and valuable comments for this book. Thanks very much.

Not the least, my thanks goes to my entire family, my darling daughter Alice, and my beautiful wife Esther. God is wonderful, thanks to all of you.

Most especially, I give the credit of this book to God from whom all mercies flow.

CONTENTS

i	Dedication	iii
ii	Foreword	v
iii	Endorsement	ix
iv	Preface	xiii
v	Acknowledgements	xv
vi	Contents	xvii
vii	Introduction	xix

Chapter 1	What is Forgiveness?	1
Chapter 2	How does God forgive?	12
Chapter 3	GOD – The Forgiver is at Work	25
Chapter 4	Ignite the Fire of Forgiveness	33
Chapter 5	Be Forgiveness Compliant	48
Chapter 6	Forward Ever	58
Chapter 7	Did Jesus Forgive Peter?	80
Chapter 8	Be Forgiving Like Joseph	87
Chapter 9	Best Practice	100
Chapter 10	What Are You Waiting For?	122

Appendix 1	134
Appendix 2	135
Bibliography	137

INTRODUCTION

Lack of forgiveness is one of the most common sins that can send any person to hell fire whether a Christian believer or not. Therefore, everyone must seek to forgive and pray earnestly that God would give them a heart to forgive, more so, a lack of forgiveness is an act of unrighteousness. And as the Bible concludes, such individuals who fail to forgive will not inherit God's kingdom, "Do you not know that the unrighteous will not inherit the kingdom of God?' 1 Corinthians 6:9a.

As a matter of fact, there must be a moment where distinct lines have to be drawn, and differences made clear regarding the standards God has set for His children about forgiveness. It is important to know that God commanded us to forgive one another and is non-negotiable. Hear what the Bible says,

> For if you forgive men their trespasses, your heavenly Father will also forgive you. 15 But if you do not forgive men their trespasses, neither will your Father forgive your trespasses. Matthew 6:14–15.

Amazingly, most of us know that Simon Peter denied Jesus Christ not once or twice, but three times, yet Jesus Christ forgave him and restored him (Peter), John 21:17. The wider implication is that Jesus Christ has demonstrated forgiveness on a human-to-human basis, and on a personal level to Peter who earlier had denied Him three times. What is expected of an individual believer is for everyone to go on and emulate Jesus' example.

He said to him the third time, "Simon, *son* of Jonah, do you love Me?" Peter was grieved because He said to him the third time, "Do you love Me?" And he said to Him, "Lord, You know all things; You know that I love You." Jesus said to him, "Feed My sheep." John 21:17.

Apart from the biblical mandates requiring everybody to forgive, there is need to consider the law of the land, and do what is morally decent and acceptable in the society you are in. Essentially, this book aims to concentrate mostly on what the Bible teaches about forgiveness and the implication(s) of not doing so, that is, lack of forgiveness, the story about the Unforgiving Servant is included for everyone to learn.

This book is a simple and easy to read material that was produced out of Sunday School sessions and my personal experiences, but it relates to one of the most challenging of life's issues that has caused some devastations, for example, death, partial or permanent medical conditions in people's lives and so on. On aggregate, the results as we discovered during the seminar, have been either overwhelming or crushing for some, or somehow less fortunate for others. Nonetheless, the most shocking revelation is the eternal consequences that we all tend to overlook like the story of the Rich Man and Lazarus as narrated in this book. Failure to forgive one another can send people to hell fire and not heaven.

In real life, there is a lady who got so close to the gate of Hell while she was in a coma at an American hospital in September 2019. The book, *Forgive & Forget - God's Love Towards Mankind* contains her story. No matter what, God wants us to forgive each other and this book provides the opportunity even though certain individual cases can be beyond the scope of this book for now, regardless every reader will gain a lot of wisdom from this book.

Reverend Dr Isaac Ajibolorunrin
Senior Pastor, Christ the Lord Tabernacle
London, UK.

CHAPTER ONE

WHAT IS FORGIVENESS?

> For if you forgive men their trespasses, your heavenly Father will also forgive you. 15 But if you do not forgive men their trespasses, neither will your Father forgive your trespasses. Matthew 6:14–15.

I started writing this chapter with some questions in the back of my mind as a result of a session of Bible Study in our local Church based on forgiveness. Some likely remarks that run through people's mind whenever we talk about forgiveness sound like, is it possible to forgive this individual "who has caused me this amount of pain?" Then they go on, "Can you imagine the level of atrocities committed after all my sacrifice and labour for him or her?" And if you are brave enough to ask them to forgive and forget, one of the responses you should expect might be, "You want me to forgive and forget? Never!" If I may ask, why can't people forgive and forget, and why is forgiveness so hard?

To be honest, it is quite difficult to give satisfactory or comprehensive response on the spot, but broadly speaking, all humans including Christian believers have to forgive as they would like God to forgive them, and also to forget about their sins. In God's view, nobody is permitted to be unappeasable, because lack of forgiveness has terrible consequences. It can turn positive when we are able to settle amicably and win our relationship back, that is, where people after realising their faults, decide to reconcile, but negative when people go their separate ways with bitterness in their heart, and the likelihood of vengeance. However, it must be noted that forgiveness is one of the essential Christian virtues in regards to justice, mercy/compassion and reconciliation which Christ's journey on earth entails, that is, from the beginning of His ministry up to the Cross when He said, "Father forgive them." Consider these two Bible passages provided below:

> Remember, O LORD, Your tender mercies and Your loving kindnesses, For they are from of old. 7 Do not remember the sins of my youth, nor my transgressions; According to Your mercy remember me, For Your goodness' sake, O LORD. Psalm 25:6–7.

In the first of the two Bible passages cited above, can you imagine the same person who wants God to forgive him or her since they were youth till date, not desiring to forgive a fellow human being? Asking God to look at them with the eyes of mercy, everlasting kindness and love and forgive them, but there is a likelihood for them to be reluctant to forgive the other person? Has it not been said that, one good turn deserves another? So why not forgive? The second Bible passage is Isaiah 64:9. How easy it is for people to want to take good care of their 'corner' but easily want to neglect others? What can this be called?

> 5 You welcome those who cheerfully do good, who follow godly ways. But we are not godly; we are constant sinners and have been all our lives. Therefore your wrath is heavy on us. How can such as we be saved? 6 We are all infected and impure with sin. When we put on our prized robes of righteousness, we find they are but filthy rags. Like autumn leaves we fade, wither, and fall. And our sins, like

the wind, sweep us away. 7 Yet no one calls upon your name or pleads with you for mercy. Therefore, you have turned away from us and turned us over to our sins. 8 And yet, O Lord, you are our Father. We are the clay and you are the potter. We are all formed by your hand. 9 Oh, be not so angry with us, Lord, nor forever remember our sins. Oh, look and see that we are all your people. Isaiah 64:5–9, TLB.

But look at God's example for us, Psalm 103:12.

As far as the east is from the west, So far has He removed our transgressions from us.

Further, in relation to the topic of forgiveness, a Minister of God commented and I agree with him, when he said, "it is sad to say, but the fact is many people find it hard to forgive, yet we offend others. Lest we forget, we are social beings; our mistakes often harm others in small and big ways. Obviously we all have suffered or inflicted offences or injuries to one another somehow, whether physical, mental or moral. The truth is everyone needs the healing power of forgiveness, and it is a must if we truly desire to enjoy forgiveness from God and to live a life that is pleasing to Him."[2]

He was right in his argument but unfortunately, many people hold their offenders in unpardonable condition for many months and years, invariably locking themselves in an avoidable imprisonment of another's offence. The consequence of doing that is simple, the person who lacks

---

[2] Pastor James Ademuyiwa, *Dose of Heaven Devotionals,* In His Presence Christ Tabernacle, London: 20 July 2020 Edition

forgiveness in their heart suffers mentally, psychologically and emotionally more than the person who offended them. The reality is a lack of forgiveness can make an individual become depressive, unnecessarily over-reactive and bitter, suffer from anxiety and if left unchecked, can turn the individual to a violent person. The Minister of God concludes, "you must work on yourself and pray earnestly that God would give you a heart of forgiveness. Forgiveness is not an option in life if you want to be an overcomer, it is an absolute necessity – you must pray for a heart of forgiveness."[3] And so what is forgiveness, what is it about?

Forgiveness – Definition

The word 'forgive' has its root in Latin and is 'perdonare' which also, is the source of the word 'pardon' in English language. To consider forgiveness from this viewpoint, would mean that forgiveness requires a person to grant a pardon to someone that offends them, it must be total forgiveness, it means to forgive completely, non-partially, and it has to be without reservation. So how can forgiveness be served correctly, bearing in mind various emotions could be involved, and bearing in mind also, that unending questions can be raised by individuals? From the look of things, can it be really true and easy to forgive completely, non-partially, and without reservation?

Humanly speaking, there has to be a bit more discussion on this. But again, forgiveness can be considered in another way. By another definition, forgiveness can be characterised as willingness to forgive, ceasing to blame someone or

---

[3] Pastor James Ademuyiwa, *Dose of Heaven Devotionals,* In His Presence Christ Tabernacle, London: 20 July 2020 Edition

something due to a fault, or granting pardon for a mistake.[4] What is interesting here is that, this last definition looks so simple and much more straightforward as defined.

Nevertheless, what can be concerning in this stance is that, the definition did not attempt to consider the state of mind of the individuals involved, the hurt suffered by any of the persons, who eventually would need support, intervention(s), or would have to take effective and necessary steps to help him or her to be restored and at the same time, try to grant a pardon to the offender. More on this later. Obviously, there is a lot to process within the shortest time on the part of the person that was wronged. Apart from being easier to say than done, the offended needs 'support' that would eventually lead to granting the offender a pardon.

Further, in order for the offended to move on, many views have to be considered. For example, are there rules and regulations that could influence choice(s) in regards to what to do, or take decision for the contrary? What observations were, or could have been taken into account prior to the incident? Additionally, what type of environment and activity were involved? Have comprehensive and careful examination(s) been carried out in order to reach a sound judgment? Are the people who were at fault the type you can see around? They cannot be seen because they are dead? Or were complete strangers? The list is inexhaustible. Moreover, assuming all due care has been taken, what outcome(s) was being searched for? Healing and reconciliation or revenge? All the foregoing questions invite our attention to some real-life issues. Are there any other way(s) to find forgiveness? But what is our take as Christians?

---

[4] J. M Sinclair, (General Consultant), *Collins Dictionary & Thesaurus*, Glasgow, Gt Britain: HarperCollins Publishers, 2000, p. 465

According to Henry Thiessen, forgiveness entails the removal of penalty for sin which *"was removed by and in the death of Christ, who bore the punishment of our sins in his own body on the tree,"* Isaiah 53:5f, 1 Peter 2:24.[5] For the reason that Christ has borne our sins, once you believe in Him, God remits the sins. That being the case, it is essential on the part of the Christian believer to go on and forgive their fellows exactly as God remitted our sins when we believe in Him.

> But He *was* wounded for our transgressions, *He was* bruised for our iniquities; The chastisement for our peace *was* upon Him, And by His stripes we are healed. 6 All we like sheep have gone astray; We have turned, every one, to his own way; And the LORD has laid on Him the iniquity of us all. Isaiah 53:5–6.

> 24 who Himself bore our sins in His own body on the tree, that we, having died to sins, might live for righteousness – by whose stripes you were healed. 1 Peter 2:24.

Not only that, the death of Jesus Christ that made forgiveness possible for Christian believers was voluntary, and it must be realised that: *"God is entitled to say on what conditions man may receive forgiveness"*[6] and not the other way round. Has anyone thought about Paul the apostle to the Gentiles, and the malefactor at the Crucifixion? There is no clear evidence of any of them struggling under the crippling effect of sin and guilt, yet see what happened to them. Through God's grace they received a compassionate pardon, so we all who profess to be Christian believers. As things are, most

---

[5] Henry C. Thiessen, *Lectures in Systematic Theology*, Cambridge: William B. Eerdmans Publishing Company, 2006, p. 276.
[6] Ibid., p. 276

likely people find it difficult to forgive and move on because they do not know how much it cost God to forgive human beings.

Regardless, God's expectation is that all humans will forgive their fellows. Unsurprisingly therefore as Lewis Smedes clearly stated, *"God invented forgiveness so that He can come to terms with a world He already knew at their best; would be unfair to each other and hurt each other deeply, and He began by forgiving us and goes on to invite us to forgive each other,"*[7] and we have to learn to forgive. Humanly speaking, forgiveness is not something that happens naturally if we really want to be honest, but being required of us by God, we have to endeavour to come to terms with it. However, one of the hindrances in this regard is our sense of fairness which if we are not careful, can push people to an extent that they see nothing wrong in failing to forgive and seeking a revenge for the wrong, or the havoc people have caused them. Can't there be another way to break this emotional pendulum or cycle? Let us hear some words of wisdom from the Bible,

> Do not say, "I will recompense evil"; Wait for the LORD, and He will save you. Proverbs 20:22.

I do not think retaliation is better for any person, preferably the appropriate thing to do is to consider how to forgive. On a better note, any attitude short of forgiveness lacks the element of grace and love, and has a tendency to undermine God's graciousness towards humanity and His merciful character, and so why won't anyone forgive? Everyone has to forgive.

---

[7] Lewis Smedes, *Forgive and Forget – Healing the Hurts We Don't Deserve*, New York: HarperCollins Publishers, 1966, pp. xv-xvi

Watch this, the same way in which once we are willing to change both in mind and intention that makes God to forgive us, so He wants us to forgive people who make up their minds and intentionally request our forgiveness. The prodigal son's story is a popular story and is a very good example at this point in time. Candidly, it shows clearly what it means to forgive and forget on God's part, despite the son's lifestyle in squandering and wasting all the resources. More so, it was wrong to ask to inherit the father while he (the father) was still alive. One of the things to be learned here is about God's way of forgiving people, which is so amazing in that, once He forgive people who sinned, the sin is deemed 'covered' and 'carried away,' this is what forgiveness meant in the Old Testament.[8] Through God's grace we too can put a lot of life's issues behind us by applying "covered and carried away" principle as in the Old Testament, which is akin to forgive and forget.

But in the New Testament it cost God His only begotten Son who had to die so that we can receive forgiveness, even as Paul narrated in Ephesians 1:7,

> In Him we have redemption through His blood, the forgiveness of our sins, according to the riches of His grace. Ephesians 1:7.

On a more significant note, the focus and pursuit of a Christian believer should be about restoring, healing a relationship that turned sour, and finding a way to enhancing the relationship. We find all these attributes in the way that the story of the Prodigal son was handled. An interesting

---

[8] David Atkinson, Contribution on Forgiveness in Robin Keeley, (Organising Editor), *An Introduction to Christian Faith,* Oxford: Lynx Communications, 1992, p. 196

twist in the story is how it opened the door for the Sonship again. Even so, such opportunity is available for anyone who is willing, but the individual has to turn to God for a taste of a richer and better life reminiscent of the lavish party as witnessed in the parable, Luke 15:11–24,

> 11 Then He said: "A certain man had two sons. 12 And the younger of them said to his father, 'Father, give me the portion of goods that falls to me.' So he divided to them his livelihood. 13 And not many days after, the younger son gathered all together, journeyed to a far country, and there wasted his possessions with prodigal living. 14 But when he had spent all, there arose a severe famine in that land, and he began to be in want. 15 Then he went and joined himself to a citizen of that country, and he sent him into his fields to feed swine. 16 And he would gladly have filled his stomach with the pods that the swine ate, and no one gave him anything. 17 "But when he came to himself, he said, 'How many of my father's hired servants have bread enough and to spare, and I perish with hunger! 18 I will arise and go to my father, and will say to him, "Father, I have sinned against heaven and before you, 19 and I am no longer worthy to be called your son. Make me like one of your hired servants."
>
> 20 "And he arose and came to his father. But when he was still a great way off, his father saw him and had compassion, and ran and fell on his neck and kissed him. 21 And the son said to him, 'Father, I have sinned against heaven and in your sight, and am no longer worthy to be called your son.' 22 "But the father said to his servants, 'Bring out the best robe and put it on him, and put a ring on his hand and sandals on his feet. 23 And bring the fatted calf here and kill it, and let us eat and be merry;

24 for this my son was dead and is alive again; he was lost and is found.' And they began to be merry." Luke 15:11–24.

In a nutshell, the Bible is unambiguous regarding the topic of forgiveness hence as stated in Ephesians 4:32,

> And be kind to one another, tender hearted, forgiving one another, even as God in Christ forgave you. Ephesians 4:32.

SPIRITUAL CHECK-UP

See if there is any offensive way in me, and lead me in the way everlasting, Psalm 139:24.

Please meditate and ask God to shine His light on your heart.

What are the likely menacing shadows that can affect your spiritual health? Ask God to show you, promise to repent and make sure you do. List them out and pray over them.

....
....
....
....
....
....
....
....
....
....
....
....
....
....

CHAPTER TWO

HOW DOES GOD FORGIVE?

This is the covenant that I will make with them after those days, says the LORD: I will put My laws into their hearts, and in their minds I will write them, 17 then He adds, Their sins and their lawless deeds I will remember no more. Hebrews 10:15–17.

Corporate institutions or establishments always have their rules and regulations to help them run their businesses properly. Also, they have their policies and procedures in which to do their work. Interestingly, it seems that people do not have problem with all that. Should any person have problems in forgiving their fellow humans? Why should any person want to do it their own way when it concerns forgiveness? It can be practically impossible for any human to have all the answers, but God has given us some instructions biblically through which people can forgive each other. How can one go about this? What is required of Christian believers is for them to study the way God forgives and emulate Him. Some of the helpful Bible passages include the following, but the list is not exhaustive, Hebrews 8:11–13; 10:15–17, Matthew 6:14–15, Proverbs 19:16, Deuteronomy 29:20. It is reassuring to know that God forgives wholeheartedly as narrated in my response to the story about the Prodigal Son. It is important to remember that the extent of prodigality was so much to warrant serious condemnation. But the conclusion is that, just as God forgives completely as demonstrated through the parable, we all are challenged to forgive and forget.

Biblical Tasters

Firstly, the New Testament states what God intended to do after Israel's disobedience which in today's context, lack of forgiveness is one of them, Hebrews 8:11–12. Anybody who fails to forgive the other person has disobeyed God and so makes himself or herself guilty before Him, in particular, reference is being made to failure to forgive here. Should anyone insist on doing what would be deemed as disobedience to God? I don't think so. As we direct our attention to the above cited scripture, it should be noted that God takes upon Himself the responsibility to put His laws in the heart of the original audience for them to know and love the laws, that way, they can start acting correctly as they should, and not for the fear of punishment from God. Presently, God has already put His laws in our minds to enable us to know Him, and His laws in our hearts to love them.[9] Therefore, no amount of argument can allow any individual to refuse to forgive the other person. Secondly, where there is inward consciousness of Christ in an individual, it won't be difficult to forgive, more so, there is the assurance of universal knowledge and God's promise of mercy regarding unrighteousness in the scripture referenced above and provided below.

> None of them shall teach his neighbour, and none his brother, saying, 'Know the LORD,' for all shall know Me, from the least of them to the greatest of them. 12 For I will be merciful to their unrighteousness, and their sins and their lawless deeds I will remember no more. Hebrews 8:11–12.

---

[9] William MacDonald, (Editor), *Believer's Bible Commentary*, London: Thomas Nelson Publishers, 1989, p. 2183

Further, it is definite that sins would be dealt with once and for all in the New Covenant as God promised His people, and refusal to forgive is one of the sins. Not only in the Old Testament when God spoke to His earthly chosen people, for example, in Jeremiah 31:30–33, but also in the New Testament, Hebrews 10:15–17.

> 30 But every one shall die for his own iniquity; every man who eats the sour grapes, his teeth shall be set on edge. 31 "Behold, the days are coming, says the LORD, when I will make a new covenant with the house of Israel and with the house of Judah – 32 not according to the covenant that I made with their fathers in the day that I took them by the hand to lead them out of the land of Egypt, My covenant which they broke, though I was a husband to them, says the LORD. 33 But this is the covenant that I will make with the house of Israel after those days, says the LORD: I will put My law in their minds, and write it on their hearts; and I will be their God, and they shall be My people. Jeremiah 31:30–33.

> But the Holy Spirit also witnesses to us; for after He had said before, 16 "This is the covenant that I will make with them after those days, says the LORD: I will put My laws into their hearts, and in their minds I will write them," 17 then He adds, "Their sins and their lawless deeds I will remember no more." Hebrews 10:15–17.

Undoubtedly, God gave His Spirit to all His children so that His law can be in their heart and mind, and His law says, we must forgive. Matthew 6:14–15.

> For if you forgive men their trespasses, your heavenly Father will also forgive you. 15 But if you do not forgive men their trespasses, neither will your Father forgive your trespasses. Matthew 6:14–15.

So far, the point I am making is that, His Spirit cannot dwell in any person at the same time they lack forgiveness in their heart, simply, the two of them cannot cohabit or be co-tenants. It is for the individual's benefit that God is asking the person to forgive. In addition, as a Christian believer, keeping His commandments is good for your soul, Proverbs 19:16.

> He who keeps the commandment keeps his soul, But he who is careless of his ways will die. Proverbs 19:16.

At this point, let us step back a little and ponder on how God forgives once again. Indeed, He forgives wholeheartedly but people need to know that forgiveness by God is not automatic, Deuteronomy 29:20. We need to be warned and not treat failure to forgive each other lightly, or as something which does not exist.

> The LORD would not spare him; for then the anger of the LORD and His jealousy would burn against that man, and every curse that is written in this book would settle on him, and the LORD would blot out his name from under heaven. Deuteronomy 29:20.

One of the implications of the above scripture is that, we are supposed to know what is good enough through the Word of God, but failure to do so becomes disobedience. It cannot be taken as ignorance. What follows from the preceding narrative is that, for you and I to be forgiven, it requires the individual to show genuine repentance, be penitent or remorseful by turning away fully, that is, three hundred and sixty degrees, (360°) from *'the sin"* (Greek, *Metanoia*). What type of sin are we talking about? The *"sin"* can be any sinful thing. However, once pardon has been granted, the person should behave as someone who earned what they did not deserve, and particularly show gratitude to God.

Additionally, talking about forgiveness, we should understand as expressed in Hebrew, forgiveness means to *'lift'* or *'carry'*[10] depicting a scenario where as if sin is either lifted off someone or removed over him or her. Being the case, it means there is an imposition in place which you have to 'lift' off, offload, or get rid of, this is what happens when you forgive someone. In other words, failure to forgive the person who has wronged you, technically means the offended is carrying a 'load' that is not meant for him or her. Too harsh? Unfortunately so long as the person remains unappeasable, he/she is carrying the 'load'.

Two Examples

First of all, it is important to realise that God wants all His children to be good Christians, but there comes a time that we are not really in good shape, or in acceptable state before God because of sin. For some reason, lack of forgiveness is one of the sins and God does not approve of it. I would like to use two illustrations to explain my point, the first is washing up liquid that we use for washing dishes at home, and the second example is, used-engine oil from an automobile or a motor vehicle. Let us recall some of the things we do at home like washing up our dishes.

Firstly some few questions, can any sane person leave their dishes in a dirty and stained condition forever? Would a sane person use some of the dirty dining plates to serve meals for themselves and their friends unwashed, many times over some days? Of course not, we know the implications, examples include, food poison, stomach ache or discomfort, diarrhoea, and so on. So it is, God does not want any of

---

[10] Derek Williams, (Ed.), *New Concise Bible Dictionary*, Leicester, England: Inter-Varsity Press, 1989, p. 176

His children to be unforgiving against one another because it has wider negative implications. We have to learn to forgive and forget, put in another way, people need to wash up the dishes and let them be clean again.

As I know, it does not cost much to buy a bottle of washing up liquid and wash up the dining plates. What would make you do that? I believe it is for hygiene reasons and your personal decision to stay clean. This is a clear case of choice. What I want to emphasise at this juncture is that you know it is beneficial for you to wash up your domestic dishes to avoid infection or food poison, so you have to decide as a matter of common sense to 'wash up' the dirt in your heart called lack of forgiveness. Do you know a lack of forgiveness is worse than leaving the dining plates over days unwashed? If you don't 'wash up' that is, if you don't 'let go,' you are exposing yourself to various health problems, most likely curable and incurable ones for that matter.

Besides, the dining plates themselves are fragile and so due care is compulsory while washing up to avoid breakage. The fragile state of human is far more complex in comparison, as an eminent writer rightly described, *"My frame was not hidden from You, When I was being formed in secret, And intricately and skilfully formed [as if embroidered with many colours] in the depths of the earth."*[11] Probably we should pause a little and ponder over this statement. Fragile? Really? Don't you think there are enough mental health patients in our society presently? The sensible thing to do is to eschew anything that can cause emotional crisis or mental health issues.

Further, I think as a result of the fragility of human nature, and mostly because we are accountable to God, we are

---

[11] Psalm 139:15, Amplified Bible Version

supposed to avoid anything that can break 'the dinner plates' or destroy our fellows through lack of pardon. So far, I chose to use 'dinner plates' as a descriptor for our heart. As a Christian believer, my appeal to you is to guard your heart exactly as the Bible says, 'Keep your heart with all diligence, For out of it spring the issues of life,' Proverbs 4:23. Don't allow your heart to be filled with a vindictive attitude. Why do you have to guard your heart? There is need to guard your heart because you want to be on the right path, particularly in life, your feelings, desire, and affections and so on, have a lot to do with decisions you make, and you don't want to make mistake. Does that mean people should not interact with others? Is there any possibility for individuals to live in isolation?

Honestly, pondering over the recent questions as a human being, it is absolutely difficult and can be daunting, because in reality we are bound to come in contact with people of different character and strange behaviours. This being the case, unless one is very careful people have a tendency to offend you whether intentionally or unintentionally. Sometimes you wonder whether our fellows have a conscience when they do, or did what certain individuals experienced. Yet, we are commanded to forgive those who offend us, if not we will not be forgiven, Matthew 6:14–15.

> For if you forgive men their trespasses, your heavenly Father will also forgive you. 15 But if you do not forgive men their trespasses, neither will your Father forgive your trespasses. Matthew 6:14–15.

The Second Example

This second example is about used engine oil from a motor vehicle. It is obvious that such *'oil'* was drained because it has already served its useful purpose. The next stage is for it to be emptied out and be replaced with a new one to enable maximum efficient performance in the automobile or mechanical device. By implication, if the used engine oil is left for longer than necessary, other parts of the engine will suffer some damage. Again, the same applies when we fail to forgive, the 'used engine oil' as a descriptor for a lack of pardon, would get to a point that it is no longer useful for one's body medically, mentally and spiritually. For short, just as other parts of the engine would suffer and not perform at their maximum capacity, so the human body will suffer, or other people in their network they associate with.

Moreover, the owner of the mechanical device or vehicle won't derive the necessary benefit(s) he or she expected, so literally the individual could become useless to themselves, other people in their lives, the same way as the used engine oil, what do you think would happen to the mechanical device? Of course scrap it or crush it. Assuming this was a human, the individual might end up medically unfit and spiritually drained, weak, backslide, or die. Worst of all, in the end, the individual would have sinned against God for carrying matters too far. It is either hell or heaven will be the result.

It is expected of you and I to go the extra mile and do the needful, this is exactly what someone who is ready to forgive would do. In a nutshell, it will cost the owner of the automobile careful planning, allocating his or her time wisely, have some money for the servicing of the vehicle, and make efforts in order to take the vehicle to the specialist. So we have to try and settle issues or take our matters to God and not keep it to ourselves.

Also, the owner of the mechanical device is mandated to operate, or drive the vehicle according to the rules stated in the Manufacturer's Manual. As Christian believers the Bible is our manufacturer's manual that we are giving to live by. Assuming your body represent the mechanical device, can you genuinely say you are using your body correctly by encouraging a lack of pardon in your heart? Interestingly, a lot of times people fail to obey God and disregard His commandment in regards to clemency. Besides, we trust the expertise of the mechanical devices of this world, but why is it so difficult to trust and obey God, the Owner and the Creator of the entire universe who created us?

Another thing 'Main dealers or Car manufacturers' technicians or mechanics do is, they use new servicing parts to do their job and offer a guarantee that in the case of any breakdown within a specified period of time, just bring the vehicle back and it would be repaired free of charge. As experts, they know they are doing a quality job with genuine spare parts, hence the warranty can be provided and we trust them. Consequent upon that, their customers have peace of mind and so they can go about their work without any worry. Why should people feel reluctant in taking their matter to God? But more than that, God wants His children to go about their obligations with good health, sound mind, and joyful heart. Here are some few references, Ezra 6:22, Psalm 16:10–11, 3 John 2.

> 22 And they kept the Feast of Unleavened Bread seven days with joy; for the LORD made them joyful, and turned the heart of the king of Assyria toward them, to strengthen their hands in the work of the house of God, the God of Israel. Ezra 6:22.
>
> For You will not leave my soul in Sheol, Nor will You allow Your Holy One to see corruption. 11 You will show me the path of life; In Your presence is fullness of joy;

At Your right hand are pleasures forevermore. Psalm 16:10–11.

Beloved, I pray that you may prosper in all things and be in health, just as your soul prospers. 3 John 2.

Drain the Used Engine Oil

All you have to do is bring yourself to Him, trust Him to heal your hurt, and learn to forgive because failure to forgive is not good for you. Additionally, be ready to let God drain out the 'used engine oil' (all traces of lack of forgiveness), which is now murky, dark and dirty, that is, the incident otherwise, the joy from His presence will not be able to find a place to settle in your heart. Further, there comes a time when the 'used engine oil' loses its syrupy nature, or viscosity, that is, its resistance properties that consistently enhance performance, and because of the lack of this essential properties, it becomes useless even though the oil is still there.

Unfortunately many Christians have 'lost it' due to failure to forgive and forget, but because they still speak in tongues, they think everything is perfect. What should be done? There is need to repent quickly before too late. In summary, it is bad enough to have an overdue, murky and dirty engine oil in your car, but it is worse if you fill your motor vehicle with wrong type of engine oil even if it was a 'new' engine oil. I have some questions for you. Since the hurt, what type of advice have you received and taken to heart? What type of approach or strategy have you adopted to dispose of the matter? Is your decision in line with the Bible? Do you know that some people could possibly be filled with wrong *'new engine oil'*? That is, wrong notions, teachings, mindset, wrong association and so on, of which they need help? Does everything look confusing to you? It is never too late to retrace your step, be hopeful and always remember that God is forever at work and forgives wholeheartedly bearing in mind the life of the Prodigal son, Luke 15:11–24, who was given a warm welcome he didn't deserve after he foolishly nursed an ambition and demanded for a premature independence.[12]

11 Then He said: "A certain man had two sons. 12 And the younger of them said to his father, 'Father, give me the portion of goods that falls to me.' So he divided to them his livelihood. 13 And not many days after, the younger son gathered all together, journeyed to a far country, and there wasted his possessions with prodigal living. 14 But when he had spent all, there arose a severe famine in that land, and he began to be in want. 15 Then he went and joined himself to a citizen of that country, and he sent him into his fields to feed swine. 16 And he would gladly have filled his stomach with the pods that the swine ate, and no one gave him anything.

17 "But when he came to himself, he said, 'How many of my father's hired servants have bread enough and to spare, and I perish with hunger! 18 I will arise and go to my father, and will say to him, 'Father, I have sinned against heaven and before you, 19 and I am no longer worthy to be called your son. Make me like one of your hired servants.' "

20 "And he arose and came to his father. But when he was still a great way off, his father saw him and had

---

[12] Isaac Ajibolorunrin, *The Nature of Grace - From the Perspective of Genesis* 6:8, London: Canada Christian College and School of Graduate Theological Studies, 2020, p. 14

compassion, and ran and fell on his neck and kissed him. 21 And the son said to him, 'Father, I have sinned against heaven and in your sight, and am no longer worthy to be called your son.' "

22 "But the father said to his servants, 'Bring out the best robe and put it on him, and put a ring on his hand and sandals on his feet. 23 And bring the fatted calf here and kill it, and let us eat and be merry; 24 for this my son was dead and is alive again; he was lost and is found.' And they began to be merry." Luke 15:11-24.

Apparently, the Prodigal Son epitomises someone who departed from his parental home (departed from God), went to a distant country (distanced himself from God and went deep into attaching himself to a lifestyle which was inconsistent to the will of God), and was totally lost in the 'new' world he found himself in, until he came back to his senses and returned home (back to God he rejected earlier). There are many options open to anyone who is willing to change from now onwards. But the wisest thing to do is to look to God in repentance and as a loving Father who is wrapped in grace and holiness, He will take the sinner back. He is always at work and ready to receive anyone that comes to Him.[13]

---

[13] Isaac Ajibolorunrin, *The Nature of Grace - From the Perspective of Genesis* 6:8, London: Canada Christian College and School of Graduate Theological Studies, 2020, p. 16

SPIRITUAL CHECK-UP

Let a man so consider us, as servants of Christ and stewards of the mysteries of God. 2 Moreover it is required in stewards that one be found faithful. 3 But with me it is a very small thing that I should be judged by you or by a human court. In fact, I do not even judge myself. 4 For I know of nothing against myself, yet I am not justified by this; but He who judges me is the Lord. 1 Corinthians 4:1-4.

Please meditate regarding the state of affairs regarding your spiritual life.

What are the likely shortcomings or faults that can affect your spiritual health? List them out and pray over them.

....
....
....
....
....
....
....
....
....
....

CHAPTER THREE

GOD – THE FORGIVER IS AT WORK

I have been crucified with Christ; it is no longer I who live, but Christ lives in me; and the life which I now live in the flesh I live by faith in the Son of God, who loved me and gave Himself for me. Galatians 2:20.

This chapter highlights a shocking revelation that beats human understanding of how God forgives when He is ready to do so. What needs to be noticed is that, when human beings become adamant or intransigent in the area of forgiveness, God can forgive the offender unquestionably because of His love for mankind. Imagine God as a loving Father wrapping His hand around the prodigal son in grace and holiness and He took him back. After such wastefulness? Assuming that was a case of a parable, has it not crossed our mind who Paul of Tarsus was? Firstly, he was a murderer who aided and was instructing them when Stephen was killed; and secondly, he was a dreadful persecutor, Acts 22:4–5.

> I persecuted this Way to the death, binding and delivering into prisons both men and women, 5 as also the high priest bears me witness, and all the council of the elders, from whom I also received letters to the brethren, and went to Damascus to bring in chains even those who were there to Jerusalem to be punished. Acts 22:4–5.

Additionally Paul was a zealous Pharisee; Philippians 3:5,[14] and someone who trained at the feet of one of the greatest and best-known educators of his time – Gamaliel,'[15] Acts 22:3, and was known by his Roman citizen name called Paul, but Saul in Hebrew.[16]

> Circumcised the eighth day of the stock of Israel, of the tribe of Benjamin, a Hebrew of the Hebrews; concerning the law, a Pharisee. Philippians 3:5.

> I am indeed a Jew, born in Tarsus of Cilicia, but brought up in this city at the feet of Gamaliel, taught according to the strictness of our fathers' law, and was zealous toward God as you all are today. Acts 22:3.

Even the Murderer And Persecutor was Forgiven and used by God!

Without doubt, the murderer and the persecutor (Paul) cited in the earlier passages was totally forgiven out of God's mercy and grace. Who was he? He was a Jew, intelligent and a brilliant scholar. Galatians 1:14.

> And I advanced in Judaism beyond many of my contemporaries in my own nation, being more exceedingly zealous for the traditions of my fathers. Galatians 1:14.

---

[14] George E. Ladd, Contribution on The Book of Acts, in Everett F. Harrison, (Editor), *The Wycliffe Bible Commentary*, Chicago: Moody Press, 1962, p. 1140

[15] Clinton L. Ryan, *Introduction to Apologetics and Evangelism*, (Compilation), p. 15

[16] Matthew Henry's Commentary – Online, p. 2, (https://www.biblegateway.com)

What could have motivated him to persecute, confine people to prison and kill? And why must God use someone who was against His agenda originally? And if God knew He would use Paul at a later stage, why should He allow the latter to support Stephens' death? Upon hearing that Paul was born again, what response would you have expected to hear from Stephen's family, the immediate fellow believers and friends who knew Paul? As you can see, the list of questions can go on, but my inclination is, God is Sovereign and He knew the end result of what He wanted to achieve before starting it. Having said that, how was Paul brought on board God's programme despite all the atrocities he had committed? How do you think people would take it when it became obvious that Paul was forgiven and now commissioned to go and preach the Gospel? Was Paul truly called by God to do the exact opposite of what he used to condemn? Acts 26:11–18.

> And I punished them often in every synagogue and compelled them to blaspheme; and being exceedingly enraged against them, I persecuted them even to foreign cities. 12 "While thus occupied, as I journeyed to Damascus with authority and commission from the chief priests, 13 at midday, O king, along the road I saw a light from heaven, brighter than the sun, shining around me and those who journeyed with me. 14 And when we all had fallen to the ground, I heard a voice speaking to me and saying in the Hebrew language, 'Saul, Saul, why are you persecuting Me? It is hard for you to kick against the goads.' 15 So I said, 'Who are You, Lord?' And He said, 'I am Jesus, whom you are persecuting.
>
> 16 But rise and stand on your feet; for I have appeared to you for this purpose, to make you a minister and a witness both of the things which you have seen and of the things

which I will yet reveal to you. 17 I will deliver you from the Jewish people, as well as from the Gentiles, to whom I now send you, 18 to open their eyes, in order to turn them from darkness to light, and from the power of Satan to God, that they may receive forgiveness of sins and an inheritance among those who are sanctified by faith in Me. Acts 26:11–18.

The Conversion, Call and Commission

From the above narrative, we notice that the Conversion and Call of Paul while he was on the way to the then chief city of Syria called Damascus, was a dramatic incident and a miracle at the same time.[17] Being the case, three questions come to mind. Firstly, was God going to use the event to shape Paul's life? Secondly, was the event a coincidence? And thirdly, was God using this occurrence to lead Paul to where He wanted? We shall see as the narration unfolds.

Paul's zeal for Judaism was responsible for the persecution and murdering of many of the members of the early Church during its infant stage. Surprisingly, he received deliverance from the power of sin during the divine encounter of the Damascus road,[18] hence Paul confesses Christ and put his trust in Him. Soon after, through divine revelation, he wrote in one of his declarations; Galatians 2:20.

> I have been crucified with Christ; it is no longer I who live, but Christ lives in me; and the life which I now live in

---

[17] Isaac O. Ajibolorunrin, *The Significance of the Church's Mission and Ministry*, (An Extract from Master's Degree Thesis), London: Canada Christian College and School of Graduate Theological Studies, May 2019, pp. 29–31

[18] Clinton L. Ryan, European Theological Seminary – *Connecting Ministry with Holy Scripture,* Birmingham: Majesty Print, 2001, p. 57

the flesh I live by faith in the Son of God, who loved me and gave Himself for me. Galatians 2:20.

It is reasonable to think that before his Conversion and Call, God was acting as if He had given Paul a long rope to hang himself, and planned 'to make this person who was the Church's Chief Persecutor to become the Gospel's Chief Proclaimer.'[19] A possible question to consider, supposed the person you think you cannot forgive was a kind of 'Paul,' what will you do if God forgives him but you failed to? We like it or not, as remarked by an eminent scholar, *"that divine encounter became a life-changing experience for Paul, and the power of Jesus Christ and Holy Ghost anointing changed his personality, purpose, and his perspective in life."*[20] The old Paul doesn't exist anymore, the sinner has become a saint, 2 Corinthians 5:17, the truth is, Paul has undergone *"a fundamental and radical change of mind, heart and action,"*[21] which meant that his life was no longer the same again.

> Therefore, if anyone is in Christ, he is a new creation; old things have passed away; behold, all things have become new. 2 Corinthians 5:17.

Have you tried to find out if fundamental and radical change of mind, heart and action have taken place in your personal life? On the other hand, supposed fundamental and radical

---

[19] Clinton L. Ryan, European Theological Seminary – *Connecting Ministry with Holy Scripture,* Birmingham: Majesty Print, 2001, p. 57
[20] Ibid., p. 59
[21] George E. Ladd, Contribution on The Book of Acts, in Everett F. Harrison, (Editor), *The Wycliffe Bible Commentary,* Chicago: Moody Press, 1962, p. 1080

change of mind, heart and action have taken place in the other person's life?

After Paul's 'Persecuting career' came to an abrupt end, Ananias who was described as a devout man, Acts 22:12-16, visited Paul because God commanded him to do so. On getting there, he prayed, baptised and relayed the message of God about Paul's commission to witness to the Gentiles and Jews to him. Nobody could have thought God would call or use Paul for any purpose, nor Paul himself would have imagined that one day he would embrace the Christian faith he was condemning. Obviously when God, the Forgiver of all sins is at work, sometimes it is difficult or impossible to understand.

> 12 "Then a certain Ananias, a devout man according to the law, having a good testimony with all the Jews who dwelt *there,* 13 came to me; and he stood and said to me, 'Brother Saul, receive your sight.' And at that same hour I looked up at him. 14 Then he said, 'The God of our fathers has chosen you that you should know His will, and see the Just One, and hear the voice of His mouth. 15 For you will be His witness to all men of what you have seen and heard. 16 And now why are you waiting? Arise and be baptized, and wash away your sins, calling on the name of the Lord.' Acts 22:12–16.

But in most vivid and impressive terms, a reputable writer perfectly remarked regarding Paul's call thus, *"when he thought that all was peace and safety, God turned a Divine Light upon him, called him by his name and said, Why are you persecuting me?"*[22] Like an offender caught in the act,

---

[22] Clinton L Ryan, European Theological Seminary - *Connecting Ministry with Holy Scripture,* Birmingham: Majesty Print, 2001, p. 59

the only choice available for Paul was to ask for mercy and seek for forgiveness from the One who is The Lord of all. Paul realising his wretched and zealous attitude being challenged, accepted the gift of Salvation which Jesus Christ offered him there and then. I am believing that any person you do not want to forgive, or are keeping malice with, will receive pardon from this moment, and may the God of all grace help to ignite your heart with the fire of forgiveness and sustain the fire for you. Please forgive.

SPIRITUAL CHECK-UP

For You are my rock and my fortress; Therefore, for Your name's sake, Lead me and guide me. Psalm 31:3

Please meditate and ask God to reveal the state of your heart to you.

What are the likely faults that can strangle your relationship with God?

List them out and pray over them and let God guide you henceforth.

....
....
....
....
....
....
....
....
....
....

CHAPTER FOUR

IGNITE THE FIRE OF FORGIVENESS

Forgiveness breaks the grip that past wrong and past pain have on our minds and frees us for whatever fairer future lies amid the unknown potentialities of our tomorrows – Lewis Smedes.

If lack of forgiveness can have strong grip on people mentally, emotionally and so on, it makes sense to say that, forgiveness should be given permission to break and destroy the grip of all wrongs and the pains associated with lack of pardon, and set one's mind free so as not to miss the fantastic future that lies ahead. In consideration of your own future and the potentialities it holds, I think the best thing to do is to initiate steps for forgiveness, or ignite the fire of forgiveness immediately. In some situations if you don't do it, nobody would like to do it for you. I am assuming that the person who hurt you would genuinely like to beg for your forgiveness, but one should equally be prepared for someone who might not sincerely mean it or necessarily care about it.

In another scenario, it could be a case of genuine intention at the beginning of the conversation, but end up causing worst harm. There is a typical example cited by an eminent writer while referring to Jesus killers, he wrote, "the killers of Jesus thought they were ridding Israel of a blasphemer, but they actually crucified the Lord with their good intention."[23] There is need to guide against a situation like this. In any circumstance, one must be positive about forgiveness and try and ignite its fire. Where do we start from? It must genuinely start from the heart.

Forgiveness Needs Time But ...

It is not really clear why individuals have tendency to break people's heart through many ways, for example, breaking trust, financial misappropriation or embezzlement, defrauding businesses, marital unfaithfulness, character assassination, deliberate spread of negative stories, to name but a few. The question we have to try and answer is, what can we do to be able to carry on in life again? To forgive? Although it might not be easy from human point of view to say a resounding Yes! but with God there is a possibility to forgive, as stated in the Bible, *"But Jesus looked at them and said, 'With men it is impossible, but not with God; for with God all things are possible,'"* Mark 10:27.

Let us start by acknowledging that it can be a challenging experience to forgive someone especially at a time when the heart is broken. Quite frankly at that point, forgiveness is the last thing you want to talk about. Notwithstanding, there are two unique instances to bear in mind. Firstly, there are those who offend you that you can see, for instance, spouses, parents, children, close friends, to mention this few. The question I want to ask is simple, will you deliberately condemn yourself to hell fire because of failure to forgive somebody?

---

[23] Lewis Smedes, *Forgive and Forget – Healing the Hurts We Don't Deserve,* New York: HarperCollins Publishers, 1966, p. 11

And secondly, will you deliberately condemn yourself to hell fire because of those you can't see any more, in all likelihood because they are dead, or were complete strangers? Bearing all sensitivity in mind, imagine where a complete stranger raped somebody and ran off? How do you handle this type of situation? It would be appalling and gruesome to hear and upsetting to bear. No sane person in their correct mind would undertake such a cruel act. Nonetheless, this is one of many tragedies in life which can be at times unavoidable, or beyond human control. Will God judge the assaulter in our absence, or set the wrongdoer free? Would we ever know God's decision regarding the culprit(s)? It is very difficult to tell but certainly there will be some consequences. This is my take, as a Christian believer, we all need to try and forgive and let God use His Sovereign power to deal with the matter as He chooses. A minister of God once gave his opinion regarding forgiveness in one of his Devotionals and I suggest we have a look at his argument perhaps some insights can be gained from the material. In talking about forgiveness, Reverend James Ademuyiwa was frank and direct in his material, he said,[24]

"Many people find it hard to forgive, however, forgiveness is God's requirement for you to obtain mercy and forgiveness from Him, typically as we recite in Our Lord's prayer, "Forgive us who trespass, as we forgive those who trespass against us," Matthew 6:12. You must forgive others if you want God to forgive you, it is a strict and fair requirement. It should be particularly noted that humans are social beings and our mistakes often harm others in various ways therefore, it is not surprising for any person to have suffered or inflicted injuries, whether physical or moral, that needs

---

[24] James Ademuyiwa, *Dose of Heaven Daily Devotional,* London: IHPCT, 20 March 2020

the healing power of forgiveness. This can be a very difficult thing for some, but a must if we truly desire to live a life that is pleasing to God. For God says, *Be ye kind to one another, tender-hearted, forgiving one another, even as God for Christ's sake hath forgiven you,* Ephesians 4:32. Also, it will be insincere for anyone to fail to be tender-hearted and forgiving when Jesus said, *And when ye stand praying, forgive, if ye have ought against any: that your Father also which is in heaven may forgive you your trespasses.* Mark 11:25.

Presently, many people hold their offender in their heart failing to forgive them for many months, even years invariably locking themselves in avoidable imprisonment of another person who do not know they have some grievance against them. The irony is that, the one who feels offended suffers psychologically and emotionally more than the person who offended them. Further, failure to forgive has made many people suffer depression, anxiety, violent anger and so on. To fail to pardon genuinely from the heart is a terrible thing, therefore it is important to pray and ask God for a heart that forgives. If we all have hearts that forgive, our world would be a better place, and there will be less animosity, killings, fewer court cases, imprisonments and less souls going to hell fire.[25]

In case you want another example to clear your doubts, I wish to remind you especially about what happened during the crucifixion of Jesus Christ. Originally, there were two criminals (robbers), who were already condemned for their crimes. There was no clear details provided about their individual criminal activities. But we know that one of the

---

[25] James Ademuyiwa, *Dose of Heaven Daily Devotional*, London: IHPCT, 20 March 2020

criminals received pardon through Jesus Christ at the point of death on the Cross, Luke 23:39–43. Considering this peculiar instance, it is dangerous to continue to remain unappeasable against any person because God might pardon the one who offended you. What would be your fate should this happen? For short, the once guilty will become the saint. To avoid a situation like that, we all have to learn to forgive. Most likely, the criminal was an unbeliever, or never attended Church meetings or fellowship, did not fast, did not pay his tithes, did not read his Bible like yourself, to mention but this few. Is it worth holding the offence against that person you don't want to forgive? Can you imagine where those he raped, robbed, killed or maimed, duped and so on, ended their lives because of failure to forgive? Would it not be inconsistent or incongruous for them to see him in heaven, but those who thought they were heaven-bound end up in hell-fire instead? Read the story;

> 39 Then one of the criminals who were hanged blasphemed Him, saying, "If You are the Christ, save Yourself and us." 40 But the other, answering, rebuked him, saying, "Do you not even fear God, seeing you are under the same condemnation? 41 And we indeed justly, for we receive the due reward of our deeds; but this Man has done nothing wrong." 42 Then he said to Jesus, "Lord, remember me when You come into Your kingdom." 43 And Jesus said to him, "Assuredly, I say to you, today you will be with Me in Paradise." Luke 23:39–43.

What to do? Forgive immediately! Unfortunately if one fails to forgive within a reasonable time, it could lead to grievous consequences, such was the case of the Unforgiving Servant in Matthew 18:22-35.

22 Jesus said to him, "I do not say to you, up to seven times, but up to seventy times seven. 23 Therefore the kingdom of

heaven is like a certain king who wanted to settle accounts with his servants. 24 And when he had begun to settle accounts, one was brought to him who owed him ten thousand talents. 25 But as he was not able to pay, his master commanded that he be sold, with his wife and children and all that he had, and that payment be made. 26 The servant therefore fell down before him, saying, 'Master, have patience with me, and I will pay you all.' 27 Then the master of that servant was moved with compassion, released him, and forgave him the debt."

28 "But that servant went out and found one of his fellow servants who owed him a hundred denarii; and he laid hands on him and took *him* by the throat, saying, 'Pay me what you owe!' 29 So his fellow servant fell down at his feet and begged him, saying, 'Have patience with me, and I will pay you all.' 30 And he would not, but went and threw him into prison till he should pay the debt. 31 So when his fellow servants saw what had been done, they were very grieved, and came and told their master all that had been done. 32 Then his master, after he had called him, said to him, 'You wicked servant! I forgave you all that debt because you begged me. 33 Should you not also have had compassion on your fellow servant, just as I had pity on you?' 34 And his master was angry, and delivered him to the torturers until he should pay all that was due to him. Matthew 18:22–35.

Prior to the above parable, Jesus was saying figuratively that forgiveness should be granted unlimitedly. It is expected that when an individual offends you, you forgive them before it turns to bitterness. The next stage is to find a way to amicably resolve the matter and as a Christian, people should be able to take it when they are rebuked. Once the individual confesses his/her sin, or admits their fault, hoping that this has been successfully done, they should be forgiven.

Wow! Unfortunately it is not that simple nor straightforward. To be honest, there is no second option but to begin your journey for forgiveness immediately, as rightly narrated by Lewis Smedes, *"Forgiveness breaks the grip that past wrong and past pain have on our minds and frees us for whatever fairer future lies amid the unknown potentialities of our tomorrows."*[26] A simple but helpful question such as follows should be asked, is it not better to seize the immediate opportunity for healing and recovery in order not to miss the chance that lies ahead?

As a matter of fact, the person's mind might be suggesting otherwise, but take decisions that will yield positive results, or that can better your life and possibly open you to a greater and better outcomes sooner. Before leaving this chapter, it is important to point out that the application of the parable of the Unforgiving Servant above is clear. All the servants had contracted a huge debt of sin that they won't be able to pay, therefore they were at the mercy of the King – God. Simply, God paid the debt in full as He was moved to show grace and compassion and granted full and free forgiveness.[27] It might sound or look strange, but it is wonderful to know that the person you said offended you, keeping malice with, you said won't be forgiven, the person you hate with passion and so on, shockingly, God loves him or her. If there are more than single individuals, God still love them, John 3:16. God would like all Christian believers to forgive any person who offend them.

---

[26] *Lewis Smedes, Forgive and Forget - Healing the Hurts We Don't Deserve,* New York: HarperCollins Publishers, 1966, p. 132

[27] William MacDonald, (Editor Art Farstad), *Believer's Bible Commentary,* London: Thomas Nelson Publishers, 1995, p. 1275

For God so loved the world that He gave His only begotten Son, that whoever believes in Him should not perish but have everlasting life. John 3:16.

How to ignite the fire of forgiveness in your heart

A lot of times, people don't know where to start from after their bitter experience, but the following eight important steps will provide you with some 'tools' to work with.

1. A lot depends on the nature of the incident, but feel free to follow the advice of the law enforcement agencies and related professionals who can suggest contacts to help you. In addition, you can support this with what your local Church can offer based on their policy/procedure in place regarding that type of incident.

2. Whether it is your fault or not, forgive by starting gradually or slowly, for example, by sharing your feelings with a good mature male/female Christian, tested and trusted friend, mentor(s), Pastor, your chosen Counsellor(s), and so on. At least let there be someone who can help to pray along.

3. Don't delay it. Start the forgiveness process with the material/contacts at your disposal.

4. There will be a time that you will feel hurt, guilty, and angry about the entire incident and so on, yet you can initiate the process because healing will eventually take place.

5. Be free to ask questions, for example, what could have influenced them to do this to me? What was likely going on in his or her life to have warranted this behaviour, etc.? But don't be too critical about yourself, instead remember that accident do happen.

6. Do a little at a time, even when your understanding of the entire incident is little, or vague. Don't rush!

7. There will be moments that one will feel overwhelmed but as a child of God, put your trust in Him wholeheartedly. Remember,

> For we do not have a High Priest who cannot sympathize with our weaknesses, but was in all points tempted as we are, yet without sin. 16 Let us therefore come boldly to the throne of grace that we may obtain mercy and find grace to help in time of need. Hebrews 4:15–16.

However, note that one of the fundamental requirements is that you need to come with a pure heart to God's presence at all times, Psalm 24:3-4, as such, let the pain-factor or hurt-factor drive you to God for your healing, and not the other way round. The other way round is to allow bitterness, malice and eventually failure to forgive to send you away from God and this is not the will of God for you.

> Who may ascend into the hill of the LORD? Or who may stand in His holy place? 4 He who has clean hands and a pure heart, Who has not lifted up his soul to an idol, Nor sworn deceitfully. Psalm 24:3–4.

8. You must be ready to swallow your pride, forgive yourself and be humble to admit your fault if there were personal contributory factors, or carelessness regarding the incident, and return to God for the needed help. An interesting story that comes to mind is found in Luke 15:14–20a,

> 14 But when he had spent all, there arose a severe famine in that land, and he began to be in want. 15 Then he went and joined himself to a citizen of that country, and he sent

him into his fields to feed swine. 16 And he would gladly have filled his stomach with the pods that the swine ate, and no one gave him anything. 17 But when he came to himself, he said, "How many of my father's hired servants have bread enough and to spare, and I perish with hunger! 18 I will arise and go to my father, and will say to him, 'Father, I have sinned against heaven and before you, 19 and I am no longer worthy to be called your son. Make me like one of your hired servants.' 20 And he arose and came to his father. Luke 15:14-20a.

Some Key Promises of God for You in this Journey

Apart from the eight essential keys to set your feet on the right channel as given above, there are five fundamental promises of God produced below for you. Hold them close to your heart and it shall be well with you.

1. Remember that God has many promises for His children which are wonderful, in particular, when challenged by issues of life, and it is appropriate to make reference to the multi-dimensional promises from God which can help as you try to forgive the person who has wronged you. For example, He says,

"When you pass through the waters, I will be with you; And through the rivers, they shall not overflow you. When you walk through the fire, you shall not be burned, Nor shall the flame scorch you." Isaiah 43:2. The cited Bible passage can be re-assuring to the heart of anyone going through issues of life. Even in that terrible state, God is still with you. In context, when you read further, you will find how God defeated great nations in order to make way for Israel in the olden times, so God will grant you victory over your own incident such that you will be able to forgive completely.

2. Always note that there is an assurance from God for you during this time, actually it is an interesting principle, and a lot of people have wondered why God decided to do that. The special dispensation has been made available because God foreknew it would be beneficial for humanity to have this provision. By this special dispensation, you are required to understand that God is ready to forgive you, and He is willing to give you every opportunity you desire. However, if you want Him to forgive you, you must first of all, forgive others as exemplified in this story, Matthew 18:23-35.

> 23 Therefore the kingdom of heaven is like a certain king who wanted to settle accounts with his servants. 24 And when he had begun to settle accounts, one was brought to him who owed him ten thousand talents. 25 But as he was not able to pay, his master commanded that he be sold, with his wife and children and all that he had, and that payment be made. 26 The servant therefore fell down before him, saying, 'Master, have patience with me, and I will pay you all.' 27 Then the master of that servant was moved with compassion, released him, and forgave him the debt. 28 "But that servant went out and found one of his fellow servants who owed him a hundred denarii; and he laid hands on him and took him by the throat, saying, 'Pay me what you owe!' 29 So his fellow servant fell down at his feet and begged him, saying, 'Have patience with me, and I will pay you all.' 30 And he would not, but went and threw him into prison till he should pay the debt. 31 So when his fellow servants saw what had been done, they were very grieved, and came and told their master all that had been done. 32 Then his master, after he had called him, said to him, 'You wicked servant! I forgave you all that debt because you begged me. 33 Should you not also have had compassion on your

fellow servant, just as I had pity on you?' 34 And his master was angry, and delivered him to the torturers until he should pay all that was due to him. 35 "So My heavenly Father also will do to you if each of you, from his heart, does not forgive his brother his trespasses. Matthew 18:23–35.

3. Remember always that forgiveness is one of God's inventions He made available ahead of time, to show by example, how to go about forgiving one another as He forgives us, the Bible states, *"But God demonstrates His own love toward us, in that while we were still sinners, Christ died for us."* Romans 5:8. It is time to prove how you can obey God's commandment by way of forgiving the person you normally would not have forgiven.

4. There is need to understand the angle through which God is coming from. Actually He looks forward to seeing all His children know Him intimately and turn a new leaf and remain children who forgive, and not children who don't forgive. Act now by forgiving the person who offended you, Jeremiah 31:31–34; Hebrews 8:10–12; 10:15–17.

> "Behold, the days are coming, says the LORD, when I will make a new covenant with the house of Israel and with the house of Judah— 32 not according to the covenant that I made with their fathers in the day that I took them by the hand to lead them out of the land of Egypt, My covenant which they broke, though I was a husband to them, says the LORD. 33 But this is the covenant that I will make with the house of Israel after those days, says the LORD: I will put My law in their minds, and write it on their hearts; and I will be their God, and they shall be My people. 34 No more shall every man teach his

neighbour, and every man his brother, saying, 'Know the LORD,' for they all shall know Me, from the least of them to the greatest of them, says the LORD. For I will forgive their iniquity, and their sin I will remember no more." Jeremiah 31:31–34.

10 For this *is* the covenant that I will make with the house of Israel after those days, says the LORD: I will put My laws in their mind and write them on their hearts; and I will be their God, and they shall be My people. 11 None of them shall teach his neighbour, and none his brother, saying, 'Know the LORD,' for all shall know Me, from the least of them to the greatest of them. 12 For I will be merciful to their unrighteousness, and their sins and their lawless deeds I will remember no more." Hebrews 8:10–12.

15 But the Holy Spirit also witnesses to us; for after He had said before, 16 "This *is* the covenant that I will make with them after those days, says the LORD: I will put My laws into their hearts, and in their minds I will write them," 17 then He adds, "Their sins and their lawless deeds I will remember no more." Hebrews 10:15–17.

5. Regardless of disobedience or unfaithfulness, be aware that God eagerly awaits the plea of His children as He pleaded with the people of Israel in the past, Isaiah 43:22–25.

"But you have not called upon Me, O Jacob; And you have been weary of Me, O Israel. 23 You have not brought Me the sheep for your burnt offerings, Nor have you honoured Me with your sacrifices. I have not caused you to serve with grain offerings, Nor wearied you with incense. 24 You have bought Me no sweet cane with money, Nor have you satisfied Me with the fat of your sacrifices; But you have burdened Me with your sins, You have wearied Me with your iniquities. 25 "I, even I, am He who blots out your transgressions for My own sake; And I will not remember your sins." Isaiah 43:22-25.

It is awe-inspiring to know that God is not keeping the score cards of our sins once we genuinely repent, and does not wish anyone to be in anguish or torment due to lack of forgiveness. The best moment to be compliant or embrace forgiveness as a lifestyle is now.

SPIRITUAL CHECK-UP

For all have sinned and fall short of the glory of God, Romans 3:23.

It's time for a soul search. Please meditate and ask God to open your eyes to your areas of inadequacy and vulnerabilities.

What are the likely weakness that can retard your spiritual progress or weaken your faith in God? List them out and pray over them.

....
....
....
....
....
....
....
....
....
....
....
....
....

CHAPTER FIVE

BE FORGIVENESS COMPLIANT

Therefore I say to you, her sins, which are many, are forgiven, for she loved much. But to whom little is forgiven, the same loves little." 48 Then He said to her, "Your sins are forgiven. Luke 7:46–48.

1. We all were great sinners before God forgave us
2. We have to learn to admit our huge guilt once upon a time
3. Forgiveness is what you need after you have been hurt or pained
4. Failure to forgive (unforgiveness) makes people carry emotional load(s) they are not supposed to carry
5. Let the load(s) fall off like it happened to the character called *Christian* in John Bunyan's book entitled, Pilgrims Progress.

From the above cited Scripture, we notice how Jesus Christ responded publicly about the woman who was a harlot. Being a harlot was supposed to be an uncomplimentary profession but that was not what Jesus accented, not because He approved prostitution, rather, He was highlighting the present state of the woman's pardon. Her past was her past, she had moved on, we all have our past, we will do well by taking necessary steps that can lead to forgiveness, and what should matter most is getting things right immediately. In her present state, Jesus said, the woman realised how much sin had forgiven her. For that reason, the woman lavished more affection upon Him from the time He (Jesus) entered the house. Further, her behaviour was in a sharp contrast to the man (Simon), the host, a Pharisee and most likely with a better professional job and a better reputation in the society at that time, and one who felt he was not a great sinner. How easy it is, to get it wrong.

Additionally, Simon did not truly acknowledge his huge guilt, and did not even had time for simple courtesy or cordial reception when Jesus first arrived.[28] Yet, Jesus went ahead and forgave him (Simon). We all need to be compliant-ready for forgiveness to be offered to people when ordinarily we think they don't deserve it. As suggested, we are all great sinners, we can all know great forgiveness and we can all love the Lord greatly.[29] Forgive.

Let the truth be told, failure to forgive is dangerous and must not be allowed to exist. What is it like? Lack of forgiveness is like putting oneself in an undeserved prison or bondage which I think is inappropriate to do, therefore, grant forgiveness to people willingly in a way that God has requested from His children, even when you think certain individuals don't deserve it. That is, consider the above example between the Pharisee and the harlot and be encouraged to comply. Amazingly, Jesus handled that occasion as a real-life situation and not a case of one of the parables He normally gives for illustrative purposes. Forgive as Jesus would do at all times.

Talking about forgiveness, it is the healing catalyst you require to steady and stabilise your life after you have been

---

[28] William MacDonald, (Editor Art Farstad), *Believer's Bible Commentary*, London: Thomas Nelson Publishers, 1995, p. 1395
[29] William MacDonald, (Editor Art Farstad), *Believer's Bible Commentary*, London: Thomas Nelson Publishers, 1995, p. 1395

hurt or pained. Why won't you forgive and be a free individual again? Sincerely, failure to pardon people must discontinue wherever God's children are. Why? The reason is when lack of forgiveness is tolerated, the person will be carrying an emotional burden or load of sin which must be allowed to fall off, reminiscent of what happened to a fictional character called *"Christian."* He was one of the imaginary beings in John Bunyan's book titled, *Pilgrims Progress*. As it happened in the play, 'the load' (bag of sin) fell off on citing the tomb of Christ and the Cross while he was walking along. Failure to forgive is like a typical bag (of sin), which must be surrendered when we come to Christ. In addition, the above remarkable turning point demands that everyone try and bring all their vexations and all that they find difficult to forgive to Jesus Christ, emphatically, all the incidents that individuals find difficult to forgive. Remember this simple, direct and clear invitation from the Bible, Matthew 11:28–30.

28 Come to Me, all you who labour and are heavy laden, and I will give you rest. 29 Take My yoke upon you and learn from Me, for I am gentle and lowly in heart, and you will find rest for your souls. 30 For My yoke is easy and My burden is light. Matthew 11:28–30.

In context, it is a dimension of important opportunity to connect with the invested authority in Christ Jesus to help anyone out, so long as they are willing. He is the best Teacher who can teach you how to totally forgive, the One whose blood removes sin's guilt, and who can help any person progress from where they are, and give eternal life.[30]

---

[30] Everett F. Harrison, *The Wycliffe Bible Commentary*, Chicago: Moody Press, 1962, p. 949

Besides, the hymn writer William Cowper (1731–1800), while referring to the atoning blood of Jesus presents us with a testimony about how Jesus' blood drawn from His vein removes guilty stains, undoubtedly lacking in forgiveness constitutes one of the stains.

> There is a fountain filled with blood
> Drawn from Immanuel's veins;
> And sinners, plunged beneath that flood,
> Lose all their guilty stains:
> Lose all their guilty stains,
> Lose all their guilty stains;
> And sinners, plunged beneath that flood,
> Lose all their guilty stains.

As is already known, without Jesus Christ all human efforts physically and spiritually put together may not go far and without any doubt, He is the One who can help to remove or ease the pressure and the daily demands of several obligations facing all human beings, which include whatever led to the incident that individuals find difficult to forgive.

As one tries to think back to the fictional character in the book titled, *Pilgrims Progress*, there is tendency for that burden, or load on the back of the actor called *'Christian'* to send or condemn him to hell fire. The saving grace was, he came across Jesus' tomb and the Cross in the play. Believably, in real life when you genuinely forgive one another's offence for the sake of God, there is the possibility that the consequences which lack of forgiveness bring about, will be removed for you without delay. However, there is only one instance in which forgiveness may be lacking or can be disallowed. The only unpardonable sin Jesus mentioned in the Bible is about blaspheming against the Holy Spirit,

Mark 3:28–29, so there is no grounds for disallowing forgiveness apart from this case. Therefore, it does not make sense for anyone to freeze himself or herself to the cruel past which lack of forgiveness is ready to confine them.

> Assuredly, I say to you, all sins will be forgiven the sons of men, and whatever blasphemies they may utter; 29 but he who blasphemes against the Holy Spirit never has forgiveness, but is subject to eternal condemnation. Mark 3:28–29.

Admittedly, the incident which affected the 'person' though vicious or reprehensible, but is now irreversible history, one should therefore be ready to forgive and move on. Although it is easier said than done, nonetheless, one's memory can be glued to the unfortunate incident to the extent that people begin to look for consequential alternatives, for example, to seek revenge. But God does not want His children to do that. Moreover, it must be understood that vengeance has tendency to cause a chain reaction and unfortunately, not everyone who starts it would see the end of it. Candidly, I think God knew ahead of everyone that the knock-on effect could be terribly bad when He said, vengeance belongs to Him so nobody should attempt to avenge anyone, Romans 12:18–19.

> If it is possible, as much as depends on you, live peaceably with all men. 19 Beloved, do not avenge yourselves, but rather give place to wrath; for it is written, "Vengeance is Mine, I will repay," says the Lord. Romans 12:18–19.

Forgiveness – A glimpse in the Old Testament

God took His time to provide mankind with forgiveness throughout the Old Testament times till the New Testament period for our good. In the Old Testament period, forgiveness for example, was associated with atonement and sacrifices which God ordained, and the key factor here was the blood of the animal that was offered, and no person was allowed to eat the blood, Leviticus 17:11-12.

> For the life of the flesh is in the blood, and I have given it to you upon the altar to make atonement for your souls; for it is the blood that makes atonement for the soul'.'12 Therefore I said to the children of Israel, 'No one among you shall eat blood, nor shall any stranger who dwells among you eat blood. Leviticus 17:11-12.

Clearly, there is nothing to suggest that the sacrifices were meant to bribe God, rather it should be viewed as a provision that a merciful God, who is slow to anger and gracious, and abounding in steadfast love provided for forgiveness, and it was God's own idea as can be seen for example, in Nehemiah 9:17; Psalm 103:8-9; Jonah 4:1-2.

> They refused to obey, And they were not mindful of Your wonders That You did among them. But they hardened their necks, And in their rebellion They appointed a leader To return to their bondage. But You are God, Ready to pardon, Gracious and merciful, Slow to anger, Abundant in kindness, And did not forsake them. Nehemiah 9:17.

> He made known His ways to Moses, His acts to the children of Israel. The LORD is merciful and gracious, Slow to anger, and abounding in mercy. 9 He will not always strive with us, Nor will He keep His anger forever. Psalm 103:8-9.

> But it displeased Jonah exceedingly, and he became angry. 2 So he prayed to the LORD, and said, "Ah, LORD, was

not this what I said when I was still in my country? Therefore I fled previously to Tarshish; for I know that You are a gracious and merciful God, slow to anger and abundant in lovingkindness, One who relents from doing harm. Jonah 4:1–2.

Forgiveness – A glimpse on the New Testament

For the sake of argument, if the above provided examples referenced in the Old Testament are not enough, a few Scriptures that can be found in the New Testament can be helpful. The references cited in regards to the New Testament, make us to understand that forgiveness can be seen multifariously through the Christ. This includes, linking forgiveness to (a) the Blood that was shed on the Cross, (b) as Christ Himself, (c) as Sin-Forgiver, (d) Forgiveness as an act of sheer grace, and (e) Forgiveness as an act of faith through grace.

A. Forgiveness is linked to the Blood that was shed on the Cross, Ephesians 1:7; Matthew 26:28,

> In Him (Christ Jesus) we have redemption through His blood, the forgiveness of sins, according to the riches of His grace. Ephesians 1:7.

> For this is My blood of the new covenant, which is shed for many for the remission of sins. Matthew 26:28.

B. Forgiveness is linked to Christ Himself, Acts 13:38–39; Ephesians 4:32.

Therefore let it be known to you, brethren, that through this Man is preached to you the forgiveness of sins; 39 and by

> Him everyone who believes is justified from all things from which you could not be justified by the law of Moses. Acts 13:38–39.

> Let all bitterness, wrath, anger, clamour, and evil speaking be put away from you, with all malice. 32 And be kind to one another, tender hearted, forgiving one another, even as God in Christ forgave you. Ephesians 4:32.

C. Forgiveness is linked to Christ as Forgiver of sins

Two instances are provided where Jesus during His earthly ministry forgave sins, Matthew 9:2–7; Luke 7:46–48.

> Then behold, they brought to Him a paralytic lying on a bed. When Jesus saw their faith, He said to the paralytic, "Son, be of good cheer; your sins are forgiven you." 3 And at once some of the scribes said within themselves, "This Man blasphemes!" 4 But Jesus, knowing their thoughts, said, "Why do you think evil in your hearts? 5 For which is easier, to say, 'Your sins are forgiven you,' or to say, 'Arise and walk'? 6 But that you may know that the Son of Man has power on earth to forgive sins"– then He said to the paralytic, "Arise, take up your bed, and go to your house." 7 And he arose and departed to his house. Matthew 9:2–7, (parallel story can be found in Mark 2:8–12, Luke 5:22–24).

> You did not anoint My head with oil, but this woman has anointed My feet with fragrant oil. 47 Therefore I say to you, her sins, which are many, are forgiven, for she loved much. But to whom little is forgiven, the same loves little." 48 Then He said to her, "Your sins are forgiven. Luke 7:46–48.

D. Forgiveness should be seen as an act of sheer grace, 1 John 1:8–9; 1 John 2:12,

> If we say that we have no sin, we deceive ourselves, and the truth is not in us. 9 If we confess our sins, He is faithful and just to forgive us our sins and to cleanse us from all unrighteousness. 1 John 1:8–9.

> I write to you, little children, Because your sins are forgiven you for His name's sake. 1 John 2:12.

E. Forgiveness is linked with Faith as a means of appropriating grace,[31] Acts 10:41–44.

> Not to all the people, but to witnesses chosen before by God, even to us who ate and drank with Him after He arose from the dead. 42 And He commanded us to preach to the people, and to testify that it is He who was ordained by God to be Judge of the living and the dead. 43 To Him all the prophets witness that, through His name, whoever believes in Him will receive remission of sins." 44 While Peter was still speaking these words, the Holy Spirit fell upon all those who heard the word. Acts 10:41–44.

If you have been able to follow the above explanations carefully, I would imagine you are now ready to eradicate all traces of lack of forgiveness, if so, you should be prepared for some new lines of propositions in the next chapter.

---

[31] Derek Williams, (Ed.), *New Concise Bible Dictionary*, Leicester, England: Inter-Varsity Press, 1989, p. 176

SPIRITUAL CHECK-UP

Hide Your face from my sins, And blot out all my iniquities. 10 Create in me a clean heart, O God, And renew a steadfast spirit within me. Psalm 51:9–10.

Please meditate and ask God to reveal your current spiritual state to you. Take the necessary action(s) once you are shown.

What did you find? List them out and pray over them. May you receive a clean heart and steadfast spirit in the name of Jesus Christ.

....
....
....
....
....
....
....
....
....
....
....
....

CHAPTER SIX

FORWARD EVER

As for you, you meant evil against me, but God meant it for good in order to bring about this present outcome, that many people would be kept alive [as they are this day]. Genesis 50:20 AMP.

Watch Yourself Smile And Move On

There comes a point in life that after a due consideration regarding what destiny has thrown at people, they have to move on because it is the best option. From the point of view of the individual above by name Joseph, one can learn a lot of life's lessons from him in relation to his thirteen years of various encounters in life. His life's journey started around age seventeen, Genesis 37:1–2, 25–28, and lasted till he turned thirty years old, Genesis 41:14–15, 46.

> Now Jacob dwelt in the land where his father was a stranger, in the land of Canaan. 2 This *is* the history of Jacob. Joseph, *being* seventeen years old, was feeding the flock with his brothers. And the lad *was* with the sons of Bilhah and the sons of Zilpah, his father's wives; and Joseph brought a bad report of them to his father. Genesis 37:1–2.
>
> 25 And they sat down to eat a meal. Then they lifted their eyes and looked, and there was a company of Ishmaelites, coming from Gilead with their camels, bearing spices, balm, and myrrh, on their way to carry them down to

Egypt. 26 So Judah said to his brothers, "What profit is there if we kill our brother and conceal his blood? 27 Come and let us sell him to the Ishmaelites, and let not our hand be upon him, for he is our brother and our flesh." And his brothers listened. 28 Then Midianite traders passed by; so the brothers pulled Joseph up and lifted him out of the pit, and sold him to the Ishmaelites for twenty shekels of silver. And they took Joseph to Egypt. Genesis 37:25–28.

14 Then Pharaoh sent and called Joseph, and they brought him quickly out of the dungeon; and he shaved, changed his clothing, and came to Pharaoh. 15 And Pharaoh said to Joseph, "I have had a dream, and *there is* no one who can interpret it. But I have heard it said of you that you can understand a dream, to interpret it." Genesis 41:14–15.

46 Joseph was thirty years old when he stood before Pharaoh king of Egypt. And Joseph went out from the presence of Pharaoh, and went throughout all the land of Egypt. Genesis 41:46.

Naturally even in good times, you would notice that after some period, people want a break, or a change from one place, or the environment they found themselves in. So in discussing about forgiveness, it is advisable to try and leave the incident behind after taking steps for healing or restoration and hopefully it gets better. Note, however that, when forgiveness has been granted or offered to someone, the person involved has to handle the matter in a way that she/he will not be experiencing the pain, hurt and all the negative effects they had in the past when the incident originally happened. As a matter of fact, flashbacks will be inevitable and it could come at any time. In reality it takes a period of time to get over such issues, and the impact and process for people getting over the trauma, differ from person to person, but the end goal is for the individual to 'forgive and forget' like Joseph said in the Scripture, Genesis 50:20.

> As for you, you meant evil against me, but God meant it for good in order to bring about this present outcome, that many people would be kept alive [as they are this day]. Genesis 50:20 AMP.

Notice that there are diverse opinions regarding forgiveness, but there is need to exercise some caution when we are told to forgive and forget as a theologian argued earlier. As he aptly postulated, *"If we forgive, we are likely to forget; and if we forget the horrors of the past we are likely to let them happen again in the future."*[32] Does that mean people should not bother themselves about forgiveness? Is the theologian saying we should not forgive and forget? What does this imply and was the theologian contradicting himself? For short, individuals have the responsibility to maintain a balance in making their judgment, for example, was the decision to forgive informed by emotions, friends, pressure, Court order, and so on? What is more, people should be able to ask themselves, "And what do I hope to achieve in the end?" But candidly as a Christian believer, the decision must be informed by the Bible, although in all honesty, it might initially look impossible to forget about the matter as if it never happened.

But no matter how bleak the outlook of things, God can be trusted for grace and strength required so that the person can get to the stage where she/he can truly forgive and forget. Quite frankly, it is a stage that is impossible to attain

---

[32] Lewis Smedes, *Forgive and Forget – Healing the Hurts We Don't Deserve,* New York: HarperCollins Publishers, 1966, p. 134

overnight. Nevertheless, one of the lessons that can be learned is that, what appeared like pain or hurt during that time, can help in shaping the present, pending and all future decisions and eventually lead to producing better results, in this vein, I would agree with Lewis Smedes' statement above. The good thing is that, the choice that people decide for, won't be chosen without a deep and proper consideration. Humanly speaking, there is a tendency for the incident to be stored in the person's memory and it can potentially last for a duration that is difficult to estimate, or it can be there throughout one's lifetime which may require different intervention. Notwithstanding, Anne Long citing Donald Coggan in her book, *Listening*, argued that, "there is no healing of the memory until the memory itself is exposed."[33] For the memory which has stored the incident to be exposed for healing, it means that the person will have to talk to someone for help. But you cannot talk to a random person, it has to be somebody you trust or a trained professional.

Points to Remember!
1. The pain today brings can become tomorrow's gain
2. Try to hang on, keep smiling and move on
3. The past pain can shape your present life— never think you have lost much
4. The pain you put behind you can help to produce better results in all your future decisions
5. Don't be afraid to share your memory, talk to someone for help
6. Be hopeful of your rising again, Proverbs 24:16a,

For a righteous man may fall seven times And rise again, ... Proverbs 24:16a

---

[33] Anne Long, *Listening*, London: Daybreak Darton, Longman, and Todd, Ltd, 1990, pp. 17–18

Help Yourself, Help Others

One clear statement that should be borne in mind is that, the affected person is out to see that she/he arrives at a point where they can forgive and forget. Six wisdom nuggets that can be ingested quickly include, (a) Open up, (b) Speak out, (c) Don't bottle everything in, it is too dangerous, (d) Keeping the incident to yourself can kill (e). No matter how bad the incident, be ready to use the experience for a better decision-making whenever required. (f) When you deem fit you can commit to raise awareness from a small to large scale, for example, having a chat over coffee weekly, organise a seminar, dropping pieces of advice on Instagram, Facebook, and so forth, to help others avoid falling into a similar unfortunate situation.

At this point, it is true to say that the longer one stores the incident in their memory, the harder forgiveness would get. Way forward, this calls for courage and a sincere resolve on the part of the aggrieved individual to turn the painful memory to God for His saving action to kick in. Further, in Anne Long's opinion and I agree, that anyone who does this will not be disappointed because God is unconditionally for us, and in her words, "waiting to loose us from what binds and burdens us, so that we can go on, not having forgotten but having had the memory cleansed, forgiven, healed, and transfigured."[34] All the same, what is required is, you have to apply positively the lessons learned from the incident for the rest of your life. All things being equal, as time goes on you will find out that when you recall the incident, or refer to the topic it never hurts like the previous times and the likelihood of pessimistic views could be minimal or zero.

---

[34] Anne Long, *Listening,* London: Daybreak Darton, Longman, and Todd, Ltd, 1990, p. 18

Presumably, one will now be left with the decision to move on, taking up the cross and follow Jesus. Having attained this level as Christ's disciple, there is no turning back on a daily and consistent basis as expressed, *"If anyone desires to come after Me, let him deny himself, and take up his cross daily, and follow Me"*. Luke 9:23. Also, Jesus said, "No one, having put his hand to the plow, and looking back, is fit for the kingdom of God." Luke 9:62. Over the last two paragraphs, it is reassuring to know that one is not a failure or a freak instead, that person can be loved by God and there will be an opportunity for a new beginning to be available again. What this means is that, although failure to forgive has effects on its victims, but people can see and walk into freedom again. Typically, an individual who comes to mind is Lysa TerKeurst and I have taken my time to produce the account of her personal testimony below. Lysa's story was narrated in Faith Gateway Today.[35] I strongly believe that the account of her experience (unedited as in below), will encourage someone struggling to forgive and forget to be challenged, and my hope is that such an individual will find help sooner. Listen to her as she narrated in *Faith Gateway Today*, a Christian electronic newsletter.

I walked into my appointment with my counsellor, Jim, wishing I'd cancelled. But this wasn't a typical hour-long appointment. It was an all-day intensive too costly to blow off. I hadn't been sleeping well. My eyes were puffy. And I couldn't remember for the life of me if I'd put deodorant on. Awesome. I wondered if the peach air freshener I'd seen before in the office bathroom could work in a pinch. I made

---

[35] newsletter@e.faithgateway.com (Cited on Sat 31/07/2021 at 16:43), *I can heal. I can forgive. I can trust God..* — Lysa TerKeurst, *Forgiving What You Can't Forget*.

a mental note to try it during our next bathroom break. I felt utterly unmotivated to talk and overly motivated to cry.

My hair was heavy with dry shampoo and tangled from a lack of proper brushing. I tried to no avail to smooth it down with my hands before twisting it up haphazardly in a top knot, fully aware I should have washed it two days ago. But who has that kind of energy when life feels suddenly emptied out in the most unfair of ways? Empty has a heaviness to it that doesn't exactly motivate one to care what they look like. "Jim, I don't know how to forgive this. He isn't sorry for what happened. Neither are some of the other people involved in this situation who also hurt me. They don't think they did anything wrong. They have no feelings around this at all.

"They are off just enjoying the mess out of life. And here I am sitting in a counsellor's office so full of hurt feelings that I wonder if it's possible for me to drown in my own tears. How can I possibly work on forgiveness when not one ounce of me *feels* like forgiving? I don't want to do this. I may be a total wreck right now, but one thing I'm not is fake."

I fully expected him to recognize that it clearly wasn't time for me to work on forgiveness and that we needed to switch the day's focus. There were plenty of other things I could clearly benefit from tackling. Personal hygiene, for example, might be an obvious choice. I don't remember what Jim said to all of my resistance. I just remember we stayed the course, and what I learned about forgiveness that day changed my life.

Jim didn't seem a bit concerned that I didn't have the desire to forgive or that my feelings weren't cooperating. It almost seemed like the intensity of my resistance made doing this exercise on this day more appropriate in his estimation, not less. That confused me. I certainly didn't want to add 'forgiveness failure' on top of everything else I was beating myself up about in this season. It was definitely time to go find that peach air freshener. When I returned, smelling like a freshly baked cobbler, Jim handed me a stack of 3x5 cards. "Lysa, do you have the desire to heal from this?" I nodded my head yes. I did want to heal. I did want to start making my way out of this pit where everything felt dark and confusing and hopeless. But I thought in order to start healing, I needed to feel better than I did about my circumstances and about the people involved.

At that point, so much felt unsettled in many of my relationships. When a person's life explodes, people around them have different reactions. You see the very best forms of compassion in most people, but not in everyone. I hadn't just lost what I thought was true in my marriage. I was also trying to navigate the shock of all the unpredictable ways people had reacted to what happened. I knew it would take me years to sort through the fallout. But, by far, the most complicated reality at that time was that I hadn't seen Art in months. We were separated. And there were layers of complicated realities that prevented us from being able to sit down together and process what happened.

How could I possibly start healing when there was no resolution or restitution or reconciliation with Art or the others who hurt me? I thought everything needed to be settled. I thought those who did wrong things would first realize they were wrong. Or, at least some kind of justice would tilt my upside-down world back in place. And something about this would feel fair. Then, I would consider forgiveness. And then I could possibly heal. But, as my counsellor kept talking, I started to realize I might never feel like things were fair. Even if every best-case scenario played out with the people who hurt me suddenly being utterly repentant and owning every bit of all they'd done, that wouldn't undo what happened. That wouldn't erase the damage. That wouldn't take away the memories. That wouldn't instantly heal me or make any of this feel right. And, chances were, most of the big situations where I got hurt were not going to play out in best-case scenarios. Big conflicts are rarely that tidy. Therefore, I had to separate my healing from their choices. My ability to heal cannot depend on anyone's choices but my own.

I remember exactly where I was standing when I finally realized what my counsellor Jim had been trying to teach me about separating my healing from others' choices. I was in Israel. It was a hot day. I wanted the guide to hurry up and finish what he was saying so we could go somewhere cooler. But then he said something that jolted me: "Jesus didn't perform very many healing miracles in Jerusalem, or at least not ones that were recorded." My whole life when I read about the miracles of Jesus, I imagined most of them occurring in and around the city of Jerusalem. I'd been to the Holy Land to study the Bible many times, but it wasn't until my eighth trip that the guide pointed this out. If you're reading the book of John, there are only two recorded healing miracles of Jesus performed in Jerusalem. One was the healing of the lame man at the pool of Bethesda, recorded in John 5. The other was the healing of the blind man at the pool of Siloam in John 9. In both cases, their healing came after a choice they made to obey the Lord, a choice not dependent on anyone else's actions. At first, the lame man thought he needed the cooperation of other people to help him get to the water when the angels stirred it, according to the superstition believed by many. So, when Jesus asked him, "Do you want to be healed?" the lame man's response wasn't "Yes!" Instead, he gave Jesus an excuse based on the fact that no one would help him get to the water.

Isn't it amazing that the man was so focused on what others needed to do that he almost missed what Jesus could do? This challenges me on so many levels. I haven't been paralyzed like this man, but I very much know what it feels like to be unable to move forward without other people cooperating like I think they should cooperate. Jesus, however, never commented about the people on whom the paralyzed man seemed so fixated. Jesus simply instructed him to get up, pick up his bed (also called a mat), and walk. The Bible then says, *And at once the man was healed, and he took up his bed and walked.* – John 5:9 ESV. The healing didn't involve anyone but the paralyzed man and Jesus.

The other miracle, with the blind man, is found in John 9. We don't read much regarding the blind man's thoughts about others around him. But we do read that the disciples very much wanted to know whose actions caused the blindness. Someone needed to be blamed. Someone was at fault. Jesus blew that assumption apart. He didn't place blame or shame on anyone. He said this man's blindness, "happened so that the works of God might be displayed in him" John 9:3. Jesus then spat onto the ground, mixed up some mud, and rubbed it onto the blind man's eyes, instructing him to go and wash in the pool of Siloam.

Jesus had compassion.

Jesus had the power.

Jesus didn't make healing contingent on other people doing or owning anything.

Jesus gave the instruction. The blind man obeyed. Jesus healed. The blind man moved forward.

Standing in Jerusalem that day, my guide continued: "In the gospel of John, there were only two recorded healing miracles of Jesus in Jerusalem. One showed us a new way to walk. The other showed us a new way to see." I'm not sure of all the nuances he intended with that statement. But for me, I couldn't grab my journal to record this revelation fast enough. And I wrote, "For me to move forward, for me to see beyond this current darkness, is between me and the Lord. I don't need to wait on others to do anything or place blame or shame that won't do anyone any good. I simply must obey whatever God is asking of me right now. God has given me a new way to walk. And God has given me a new way to see. It's forgiveness. And it is beautiful." I have to place my healing in the Lord's hands. I need to focus on what I can do to step toward Him in obedience. And forgiveness is what He's asking of me. I must separate my healing from others' repentance or lack thereof. My ability to heal cannot be conditional on them wanting my forgiveness but only on my willingness to give it.

And I have to separate my healing from any of this being fair. My ability to heal cannot be conditional on the other person receiving adequate consequences for their disobedience but only on my obedience to trust God's justice whether I ever see it or not.

My healing is my choice. I can heal. I can forgive. I can trust God. And none of those beautiful realities are held hostage by another person. Healing will take time. But I must move forward toward it if I ever hope to get there. And forgiveness is a good step in the right direction. Not just good, but necessary.[36]

Effects of Forgiveness

Forgiveness gives opportunity or places you in a position in which your entire life can be seen in a new way again, but it does not mean the problem or scar has left completely. For example, there will be such issues as guilt, blame, shame, and self-condemnation, mental and psychological challenges to grapple with. As rightly asserted by Derek Tidball, "many will still struggle with self-condemnation and others will continue to wrestle with psychological difficulties" for some time.[37] Not only self-condemnation, but there is also a likelihood of suffering from self-guilt, thoughts of not living up to expectations, letting God down, self-unworthiness, and self-inferiority to mention this few. Further, it seems to me that there is truth in Derek Tidball's argument when he said, "it sometimes seems easier to believe that God has forgiven us than it is to forgive ourselves"[38] strange as it might sound, but it is there in His Word how God forgives as soon as one genuinely ask Him for forgiveness, Isaiah 43:25.

> I, even I, am He who blots out your transgressions for My own sake; And I will not remember your sins. Isaiah 43:25.

---

[36] Faith Gateway Today <newsletter@e.faithgateway.com> Sat 31/07/2021 16:43
I can heal. I can forgive. I can trust God.. — Lysa TerKeurst, *Forgiving What You Can't Forget*
[37] Derek J. Tidball, *Skillful Shepherd – Explorations in Pastoral Theology*, Leicester: Inter-Varsity Press, 1997, p. 274
[38] Derek J. Tidball, *Skillful Shepherd – Explorations in Pastoral Theology*, Leicester: Inter-Varsity Press, 1997, p. 274

On the other hand, I submit firstly, that forgiveness does not necessarily take away, or eliminate the consequences of the wrong actions. Secondly, it does not restore one's innocence, or the psychological injury which was inflicted on someone. However, what should matter is, if God has concluded that the matter is closed, why should the incident be put back in that person's mind? It should be emphasised that one of the destructive implications in this regard is self-condemnation. As rightly asserted by the eminent scholar, "self-condemning memory can be disabling and lead to a sense of inferiority which prevents us from being the true sons of God and keeps us as slaves in His house," Galatians 3:26–4:7."[39] But we are God's sons and daughters therefore, we have to make forgiveness a top priority and not to be held as slaves in bondage because of failure to forgive.

> 26 For you are all sons of God through faith in Christ Jesus. 27 For as many of you as were baptized into Christ have put on Christ. 28 There is neither Jew nor Greek, there is neither slave nor free, there is neither male nor female; for you are all one in Christ Jesus. 29 And if you are Christ's, then you are Abraham's seed, and heirs according to the promise. Galatians 3:26–29.

> 1 Now I say that the heir, as long as he is a child, does not differ at all from a slave, though he is master of all, 2 but is under guardians and stewards until the time appointed by the father. 3 Even so we, when we were children, were in bondage under the elements of the world. 4 But when the fullness of the time had come, God sent forth His Son, born of a woman, born under the law, 5 to redeem those

---

[39] Derek J. Tidball, *Skillful Shepherd – Explorations in Pastoral Theology*, Leicester: Inter-Varsity Press, 1997, p. 275

who were under the law, that we might receive the adoption as sons. 6 And because you are sons, God has sent forth the Spirit of His Son into your hearts, crying out, "Abba, Father!" 7 Therefore you are no longer a slave but a son, and if a son, then an heir of God through Christ. Galatians 4:1–7.

Furthermore, the Prodigal son's story can serve as a good reference, Luke 15:17–24.

17 But when he came to himself, he said, 'How many of my father's hired servants have bread enough and to spare, and I perish with hunger! 18 I will arise and go to my father, and will say to him, "Father, I have sinned against heaven and before you, 19 and I am no longer worthy to be called your son. Make me like one of your hired servants." 20 "And he arose and came to his father. But when he was still a great way off, his father saw him and had compassion, and ran and fell on his neck and kissed him. 21 And the son said to him, 'Father, I have sinned against heaven and in your sight, and am no longer worthy to be called your son.' 22 "But the father said to his servants, 'Bring out the best robe and put it on him, and put a ring on his hand and sandals on his feet. 23 And bring the fatted calf here and kill it, and let us eat and be merry; 24 for this my son was dead and is alive again; he was lost and is found.' And they began to be merry. Luke 15:17–24.

Observation

It should be realised that the Prodigal son was forgiven when he returned home, but the huge amount of money he took away was gone! He lavished them recklessly and there was no way the money could return back to the bank account. Additionally, he had a broken relationship with his brother pending. Notwithstanding, irrespective of the unpalatable experience he subjected himself to, and other negative effects, it is heart-warming to know that the Bible provides us with physical and psychological healing, which was accorded the Prodigal son, and is available to anyone who is willing to have it, but this is not meant to promote or encourage indulgence. Some scriptures for encouragement, Psalms 41:3–4; 103:2–3; 147:2–3; Isaiah 57:18–19.

> The LORD will strengthen him on his bed of illness; You will sustain him on his sickbed. 4 I said, "LORD, be merciful to me; Heal my soul, for I have sinned against You." Psalm 41:3–4.
>
> Bless the LORD, O my soul, And forget not all His benefits: 3 Who forgives all your iniquities, Who heals all your diseases. Psalm 103:2–3.
>
> The LORD builds up Jerusalem; He gathers together the outcasts of Israel. 3 He heals the broken hearted And binds up their wounds. Psalm 147:2–3.
>
> 18 I have seen his ways, and will heal him; I will also lead him, And restore comforts to him And to his mourners. 19 "I create the fruit of the lips: Peace, peace to him who is far off and to him who is near," Says the LORD, "And I will heal him." Isaiah 57:18–19.

Twelve Principles to Aid Your Journey To Freedom

You can begin the journey to your freedom from this moment by making the decision to break the shackles of lack of forgiveness. Try the following principles:

1. Start by forgiving yourself, forgive all the people involved, or who had some roles to play in the incident. You need to do this because Jesus forgave you in order for you to forgive yourself and others, Matthew 6:10-12; 18:23-35.

> 10 Your kingdom come. Your will be done On earth as it is in heaven. 11 Give us this day our daily bread. 12 And forgive us our debts, As we forgive our debtors. Matthew 6:10–12.

> 23 Therefore the kingdom of heaven is like a certain king who wanted to settle accounts with his servants. 24 And when he had begun to settle accounts, one was brought to him who owed him ten thousand talents. 25 But as he was not able to pay, his master commanded that he be sold, with his wife and children and all that he had, and that payment be made. 26 The servant therefore fell down before him, saying, 'Master, have patience with me, and I will pay you all.' 27 Then the master of that servant was moved with compassion, released him, and forgave him the debt. 28 "But that servant went out and found one of his fellow servants who owed him a hundred denarii; and he laid hands on him and took him by the throat, saying, 'Pay me what you owe!' 29 So his fellow servant fell down at his feet and begged him, saying, 'Have patience with me, and I will pay you all.' 30 And he would not, but went and threw him into prison till he should pay the debt. 31 So when his fellow servants saw what had been done, they were very grieved, and came and told their master all that had been done. 32 Then his master, after he had called him, said to him, 'You wicked servant! I forgave you all that debt because you begged me. 33 Should you not also have had compassion on your fellow servant, just as I had pity on you?' 34 And his master was angry, and delivered him to the torturers until

he should pay all that was due to him. 35 "So My heavenly Father also will do to you if each of you, from his heart, does not forgive his brother his trespasses." Matthew18:23–35.

2. Look for, listen to and befriend those who have genuinely forgiven people who offended them, and learn from such individuals and apply from their shared wisdom any suitable wisdom/strategy that can help you. For example, you can read again Lysa TerKeurst's story as provided above.

3. Never deny the pain that comes through hurts after you have been wronged, but avail yourself of tools/strategy/therapy that can heal you, such as, talking to trusted Christian adults, contacting relevant professional authorities, reading relevant Bible passages, that can promote healing/recovery in regards to the incident. In addition, note that forgiveness might not restore the innocence, or erase the memory of the incident immediately, but if God has declared us forgiven and has called us His sons and daughters, no one should put the agenda of the incident back on their minds to enslave the person again, Galatians 3:26-29; 4:6–7.

> 26 For you are all sons of God through faith in Christ Jesus. 27 For as many of you as were baptized into Christ have put on Christ. 28 There is neither Jew nor Greek, there is neither slave nor free, there is neither male nor female; for you are all one in Christ Jesus. 29 And if you are Christ's, then you are Abraham's seed, and heirs according to the promise. Galatians 3:26–29.

> 6 And because you are sons, God has sent forth the Spirit of His Son into your hearts, crying out, "Abba, Father!" 7 Therefore you are no longer a slave but a son, and if a son, then an heir of God through Christ. Galatians 4:6–7.

4. Take wise counsel from mature Christians/Ministers of God you can trust, or attend relevant Counselling sessions as soon as possible because it is good for your health in general, Proverbs 11:14.

> Where there is no counsel, the people fall; But in the multitude of counsellors there is safety. Proverbs 11:14.

5. Talk to someone who has suffered the same fate before, but not only that, try and listen to helpful CDs, DVDs and read relevant books about your circumstance and gain some wisdom, Proverbs 24:6.

> For by wise counsel you will wage your own war, And in a multitude of counsellors there is safety. Proverbs 24:6.

6. The role that the Holy Spirit can play in your 'Recovery Plan' cannot be over-emphasised, but you have to allow Him to minister to your heart, Psalm 32:8; John 14:26.

> I will instruct you and teach you in the way you should go; I will guide you with My eye. Psalm 32:8.

> 26 But the Helper, the Holy Spirit, whom the Father will send in My name, He will teach you all things, and bring to your remembrance all things that I said to you. John 14:26.

7. You should always remember the Redemptive work of God and retain only good memories — exactly as the Israelites were instructed to forget the past horrors of slavery and bondage in Egypt, but to keep only good memories as stated in Exodus 12 :23–28.

23 For the LORD will pass through to strike the Egyptians; and when He sees the blood on the lintel and on the two doorposts, the LORD will pass over the door and not allow the destroyer to come into your houses to strike you. 24 And you shall observe this thing as an ordinance for you and your sons forever. 25 It will come to pass when you come to the land which the LORD will give you, just as He promised, that you shall keep this service. 26 And it shall be, when your children say to you, 'What do you mean by this service?' 27 that you shall say, 'It is the Passover sacrifice of the LORD, who passed over the houses of the children of Israel in Egypt when He struck the Egyptians and delivered our households.' " So the people bowed their heads and worshiped. 28 Then the children of Israel went away and did so; just as the LORD had commanded Moses and Aaron, so they did. Exodus 12 :23–28.

8. It is helpful to constantly remind yourself of the consequences of lack of forgiveness like medical and spiritual complications that can happen, for that reason, begin to prevent yourself from drifting towards anger, bitterness, or mental health illness.

9. "You have to let go!" – You have to come to a conclusion that you want your life back. Also, that you want your prayers to be answered, and as such forgetting about the assault is non-negotiable as said by the Psalmist, Psalm 66:16-20.

> Come and hear, all you who fear God, And I will declare what He has done for my soul. 17 I cried to Him with my mouth, And He was extolled with my tongue. 18 If I regard iniquity in my heart, The Lord will not hear.

19 But certainly God has heard me; He has attended to the voice of my prayer. 20 Blessed be God, Who has not turned away my prayer, Nor His mercy from me! Psalm 66:16–20.

10. Consciously develop an unlimited appetite for the Word of God even when you don't feel like reading it. As a matter of fact, it is not an option, as soon as you sense that you are finding it difficult to forgive, I advise you to get a good Bible some of them have reference pages or subject index, and check for related Bible passages on forgiveness to caution you, broaden your knowledge, or remind you about what God expects of you, Psalm 1:1-2, 119:10-12.

1 Blessed is the man Who walks not in the counsel of the ungodly, Nor stands in the path of sinners, Nor sits in the seat of the scornful; 2 But his delight is in the law of the LORD, And in His law he meditates day and night. Psalm 1:1-2.

10 With my whole heart I have sought You; Oh, let me not wander from Your commandments! 11 Your word I have hidden in my heart, That I might not sin against You. 12 Blessed are You, LORD! Teach me Your statutes. Psalm 119:10-12.

11. You have to avoid the temptation of "forgiving and forgetting some, but keeping some" – Forgive all, forget all lest it becomes an 'idol' in your heart, Psalm 24:3-4.

Who may ascend into the hill of the LORD? Or who may stand in His holy place?4 He who has clean hands and a pure heart, Who has not lifted up his soul to an idol, Nor sworn deceitfully. Psalm: 24:3–4.

12. Be selective in what you want to keep or retain in your heart, fix your thoughts on what is good, what you can praise God for, and what can make you glad, as expressed in, Philippians 4:8.

> Finally, brethren, whatever things are true, whatever things are noble, whatever things are just, whatever things are pure, whatever things are lovely, whatever things are of good report, if there is any virtue and if there is anything praiseworthy – meditate on these things. Philippians 4:8.

If you can put the majority of the above twelve principles into practice, you have delivered yourself from mental health difficulties. Again, the above stated points are testimony to the fact that, the sufferer can be relieved of their psychological difficulties resulting from forgiveness they offer to the offender. Not only that, but also, it provides the needed courage to face the difficulties and challenges originally caused by the incident. Thus any person who forgives, is in actual fact is helping himself or herself.

SPIRITUAL CHECK-UP

For all have sinned and fall short of the glory of God, Romans 3:23.

Nobody is perfect. Please meditate and ask God to conduct a divine search on your heart and show what should be uprooted and dumped from your life immediately.

What are the likely imperfections that can retard your spiritual progress? List them out and pray over them.

....
....
....
....
....
....
....
....
....
....
....
....
....
....

CHAPTER SEVEN

DID JESUS FORGIVE PETER?

Simon who was surnamed Peter, Matthew 16:17–18, at a particular time in Jesus' ministry raises some questions regarding how he behaved towards Jesus Christ, did he behave correctly and do you think Jesus forgave him?

> 17 Jesus answered and said to him, "Blessed are you, Simon Bar-Jonah, for flesh and blood has not revealed this to you, but My Father who is in heaven. 18 And I also say to you that you are Peter, and on this rock I will build My church, and the gates of Hades shall not prevail against it. Matthew 16:17–18.

Have you seen people show wisdom beyond human capacity before? Can a born-again Christian backslide? How possible and when? Although the above scripture carries the historic confession about Israel's messiah and the testimony that Christ is the Son of God as Peter confessed it at the time. This confession was beyond human wisdom or intellect and Jesus commended the source as being through supernatural revelation. All these appear great on Peter's curriculum vitae or profile, but in addition to that, a blessing was pronounced on him, when he was surnamed Peter (now Simon Peter), instead of Simon Bar-Jonah he was known as from the beginning. Would anyone think such a person can deny Jesus? However, it was predicted by Jesus as stated in John 13:37–38.

> 37 Peter said to Him, "Lord, why can I not follow You now? I will lay down my life for Your sake." 38 Jesus answered him, "Will you lay down your life for My sake? Most assuredly, I say to you, the rooster shall not crow till you have denied Me three times. John 13:37–38.

In other words, what message was Jesus trying to pass across on this occasion in particular with Peter when the betrayal was pending? To start with, it is possible that the denial was not believed by the original audience, or at least Peter himself did not believe he would do that especially, as he is known for his enthusiasm and his willingness to lay down his life for his Master, that is Jesus. In regards to the prediction, what in today's world do you think should have been done ? Possible options include, fasting and prayers to solicit for God's mercy and intervention like in Daniel 2:11-19, and so on.

The Prediction is Fulfilled!

> 16 But Peter stood at the door outside. Then the other disciple, who was known to the high priest, went out and spoke to her who kept the door, and brought Peter in. 17 Then the servant girl who kept the door said to Peter, "You are not also one of this Man's disciples, are you?" He said, "I am not" John 18:16–17.

> 25 Now Simon Peter stood and warmed himself. Therefore they said to him, "You are not also one of His disciples, are you?" He denied it and said, "I am not!" 26 One of the servants of the high priest, a relative of him whose ear Peter cut off, said, "Did I not see you in the garden with Him?" 27 Peter then denied again; and immediately a rooster crowed. John 18:25–27.

As can be deduced from the above situation, like Peter, no person can follow the Lord in their own power and strength. Amongst others, human intelligence is good, but we need divine knowledge to help us know more than what one's immediate circumstance or environment looks like, or can turn out to be, in particular, to have strength and courage to face dire situations – for they will surely come. Truth be told, it is supposed to be humanly impossible to experience all that Peter did to Jesus especially when he denied the latter three times and still keep such a person on your team, Board of Trustees, or retain the individual as one of your directors if in business, and even trust him with a bigger responsibility. To some of us in today's world, it would be weird to do so, but not like that with God. As you read along, you will be able to see how Jesus forgave Peter and forgot about the wrongs resulting from the denial, He did it all because of His love towards mankind and understandably not just to Peter alone. Of course, Peter was martyred but that took place some years later when he had overcome cowardice and human weakness as we read above, John 18:16–17, 25–27. For the sake of good practise, we must think beyond our immediate circumstance or beyond now, project into the future positively as nobody knows tomorrow.

Forgiveness → Restoration → Task

Although Peter denied Jesus but the redemption plan of God has a role to play in this matter yet, it must be understood that Jesus while in human flesh could have felt disappointed if not for the fact that as the Son of God, He had known the ending from the beginning. Notwithstanding, much as restoration stands out clearly in the Scripture, John 21:15–17, definitely Peter was forgiven before he was restored. Then he was given a task when he was told to feed the lambs and the sheep.

> 15 So when they had eaten breakfast, Jesus said to Simon Peter, "Simon, son of Jonah, do you love Me more than these?" He said to Him, "Yes, Lord; You know that I love You." He said to him, "Feed My lambs." 16 He said to him again a second time, "Simon, son of Jonah, do you love Me?" He said to Him, "Yes, Lord; You know that I love You." He said to him, "Tend My sheep." 17 He said to him the third time, "Simon, son of Jonah, do you love Me?" Peter was grieved because He said to him the third time, "Do you love Me?" And he said to Him, "Lord, You know all things; You know that I love You." Jesus said to him, Feed My sheep. John 21:15–17.

Surprisingly, one may wonder the reference to the name – Simon Bar-Jonah in the text. This is a reminder of Peter's fallen state earlier, he lost the plot like king Saul in (1 Samuel 16:1) fortunately for him, he wasn't rejected like Saul the king, which meant he was allowed to keep his given-name 'Simon Peter' the surname which was given by Jesus to him. Nonetheless, he remains the 'Simon Peter' the surname which was given by Jesus to him around the time of the revelation on the mount of Transfiguration, Matthew 16:14–18.

Further, this peculiar act clearly shows Jesus as teaching us how to forgive unconditionally and completely. Also, it is important to remember that before taking care of the spiritual, Jesus took care of their physical needs by preparing the breakfast. Interestingly, Peter who denied his Master three times publicly, is called three times publicly to kick-start his restoration process. This was necessary so that he would command respect among the fellow disciples and nobody would cast any doubt about Peter's leadership position when later he would be carrying out the assigned tasks the Lord gave him. All the same, what does the statement, "feed My lambs and My sheep mean?" There is an interesting twist here, in that the topic is changing from fishing to feeding Jesus' lambs and sheep. To recall, the reference we heard in the past was 'follow Me and I will make you fishers of men,' which refers to the works of evangelism, Matthew 4:18–20.

> 18 And Jesus, walking by the Sea of Galilee, saw two brothers, Simon called Peter, and Andrew his brother, casting a net into the sea; for they were fishermen. 19 Then He said to them, "Follow Me, and I will make you fishers of men." 20 They immediately left their nets and followed Him. Matthew 4:18–20.

The reason for Jesus' decision when He changed the topic from 'fishing to feeding' can be attributed to compassion and grace and never a sign of weak leadership. We all need these two important elements (compassion and grace) from time to time in our decision making.

From Evangelism to Loving and Pastoral Care

But now, the new task is about 'feeding the lambs' which calls for demonstrating Christ's love by teaching and giving pastoral care to the young ones. Of course, the 'sheep' or the adults equally deserve the loving care of Jesus Christ. To conclude, the only motive for serving the Lord in any capacity should be based on the love we have for Him,[40] because while we were still sinners He died for us, Romans 5:7–8.

> 7 For scarcely for a righteous man will one die; yet perhaps for a good man someone would even dare to die.

---

[40] William MacDonald, (Editor Art Farstad), *Believer's Bible Commentary*, London: Thomas Nelson Publishers, 1995, p. 1571

8 But God demonstrates His own love toward us, in that while we were still sinners, Christ died for us. Romans 5:7–8.

It should also, be borne in mind that Jesus teaches us to forgive unconditionally and completely through how He treated Peter simply, He shows that there was no need to remain unforgiving. Unfortunately, people tend to hold what individuals did against them at heart, and at times vow that those who offended/hurt them would never be forgiven. I have a question, if you were in Jesus' shoes would you have forgiven Peter? As a reminder, failure to forgive is one of the sins that can send people to hell fire including any careless Christian believer. Can you afford that? This is why it is important for everyone to work on themselves and pray earnestly that God would give them a heart of forgiveness. Candidly, lack of forgiveness is an act of unrighteousness and as the Bible concludes, such individuals will not inherit God's kingdom, as it reads, 'Know ye not that the unrighteous shall not inherit the kingdom of God?' 1 Corinthians 6:9a.[41] In reality, many people would have died without forgiving Peter if they were in Jesus' shoes. But He (Jesus) chose to forgive Peter so that He can show us that failure to forgive is dishonourable and deadlier.

---

[41] James Ademuyiwa, *Dose of Heaven Daily Devotional*, London: IHPCT, 20 March 2020, Edition.

SPIRITUAL CHECK-UP

O Lord, to us belongs shame of face, to our kings, our princes, and our fathers, because we have sinned against You. 9 To the Lord our God belong mercy and forgiveness, though we have rebelled against Him, Daniel 9:8–9.

Pray, meditate, and ask the Holy Spirit to produce the true picture of yourself so you can make all the necessary amends. What are the likely shortcomings that can retard your spiritual progress? List them out and pray over them.

....
....
....
....
....
....
....
....
....
....
....
....
....
....

CHAPTER EIGHT

BE FORGIVING LIKE JOSEPH

Most of the biblical characters had the blessings of God resting on their lives, however, it didn't exclude them from life's troubles – Isaac Ajibolorunrin

General Background

It is not an exaggeration to say that most of the biblical characters had the blessings of God resting on their lives, at least, a reference can be made to one of them called Joseph, who was the son of Jacob, Genesis 35:11–14, 22b–26, and it was through this Joseph's father that the covenant inheritance was handed as one of the descendants of Abraham as mentioned in, Genesis 12:7–9.

> 11 Also God said to him: "I am God Almighty. Be fruitful and multiply; a nation and a company of nations shall proceed from you, and kings shall come from your body. 12 The land which I gave Abraham and Isaac I give to you; and to your descendants after you I give this land." 13 Then God went up from him in the place where He talked with him. 14 So Jacob set up a pillar in the place where He talked with him, a pillar of stone; and he poured a drink offering on it, and he poured oil on it. Genesis 35:11–14.

Now the sons of Jacob were twelve: 23 the sons of Leah were Reuben, Jacob's first born, and Simeon, Levi, Judah,

Issachar, and Zebulun; 24 the sons of Rachel were Joseph and Benjamin; 25 the sons of Bilhah, Rachel's maidservant, were Dan and Naphtali; 26 and the sons of Zilpah, Leah's maidservant, were Gad and Asher. These were the sons of Jacob who were born to him in Padan Aram. Genesis 35:22b-26.

> 7 Then the LORD appeared to Abram and said, "To your descendants I will give this land." And there he built an altar to the LORD, who had appeared to him. 8 And he moved from there to the mountain east of Bethel, and he pitched his tent with Bethel on the west and Ai on the east; there he built an altar to the LORD and called on the name of the LORD. 9 So Abram journeyed, going on still toward the South. Genesis 12:7–9.

To be quite clear, this Joseph under discussion was the grandson of Isaac, and he (Joseph) was fortunate to be the great grandson of Abraham who was the friend of God, Isaiah 41:8–9.

> But you, Israel, are My servant, Jacob whom I have chosen, The descendants of Abraham My friend. 9 You whom I have taken from the ends of the earth, And called from its farthest regions, And said to you, 'You are My servant, I have chosen you and have not cast you away. Isaiah 41:8–9.

Hypothetically, think of a world where your grandparent was a friend of the President of the most powerful nation of this world. Can anyone imagine the privileges, opportunities, connections and contacts that would be available to the person? All that the individual presumably would need is a telephone call, or send an email to the related offices and things would get done. What a world! The good news is, there is a God who is greater than all the Presidents of this world combined, including the most powerful and influential heads of government of this world, and we all have access to Him except those who refuse His invitation to be part of His special family. He says, in, Revelation 3:20 and Matthew 11:28.

> 20 Behold, I stand at the door and knock. If anyone hears My voice and opens the door, I will come in to him and dine with him, and he with Me. Revelation 3:20.

> 28 Come to Me, all you who labour and are heavy laden, and I will give you rest. Matthew 11:28.

Animosity, hatred and sibling rivalry, will the dream come true?

Recalling a bit about Joseph's personal background will give insight about the extent of animosity, vulnerability, sibling rivalry, Genesis 37:18–20, harassment and physical abuse which he suffered, Genesis 37:23–24, then finally he was sold as a slave to Egypt, Genesis 37:27–28. For a moment the fulfilment of the revelatory dreams he had some time ago remain hanging, Genesis 37:5–11.

> 18 Now when they saw him afar off, even before he came near them, they conspired against him to kill him. 19 Then they said to one another, "Look, this dreamer is coming! 20 Come therefore, let us now kill him and cast him into some pit; and we shall say, 'Some wild beast has devoured him.' We shall see what will become of his dreams!" Genesis 37:18–20.

> 23 So it came to pass, when Joseph had come to his brothers, that they stripped Joseph of his tunic, the tunic

of many colours that was on him. 24 Then they took him and cast him into a pit. And the pit was empty; there was no water in it. Genesis 37:23-24.

27 Come and let us sell him to the Ishmaelites, and let not our hand be upon him, for he is our brother and our flesh." And his brothers listened. 28 Then Midianite traders passed by; so the brothers pulled Joseph up and lifted him out of the pit, and sold him to the Ishmaelites for twenty shekels of silver. And they took Joseph to Egypt. Genesis 37:27-28.

5 Now Joseph had a dream, and he told it to his brothers; and they hated him even more. 6 So he said to them, "Please hear this dream which I have dreamed: 7 There we were, binding sheaves in the field. Then behold, my sheaf arose and also stood upright; and indeed your sheaves stood all around and bowed down to my sheaf." 8 And his brothers said to him, "Shall you indeed reign over us? Or shall you indeed have dominion over us?" So they hated him even more for his dreams and for his words. 9 Then he dreamed still another dream and told it to his brothers, and said, "Look, I have dreamed another dream. And this time, the sun, the moon, and the eleven stars bowed down to me." 10 So he told it to his father and his brothers; and his father rebuked him and said to him, "What is this dream that you have dreamed? Shall your mother and I and your brothers indeed come to bow down to the earth before you?" 11 And his brothers envied him, but his father kept the matter in mind. Genesis 37:5-11.

Attack such as envy, jealousy and sibling rivalry from blood relations did not prevent God's plan for Joseph from happening. But soon, another temptation would come.

Sexual temptation and adversity, can forgiveness make sense?

Normally, where someone was a victim of lies, adversity and sexually accused of an uncommitted crime and remanded into prison custody, to forgive the perpetrators can be difficult. But not really so with Joseph. He must be credited for his wisdom in handling the sexual temptation. He did not succumb to the pressure and the temptation which was piled on him persistently. What was his secret? Most likely, his personal knowledge of God, his pain which shaped him, and his ability to draw strength from whatever confronted him throughout the time of his adversity played a major role.

Most of all, he chose to handle every setback that happened to him positively and forgave all the people who wronged him at the end of his hardship, Genesis 50:16–21. Is it really fair to be punished with imprisonment for at least two years, for doing the right thing? Or go through hardships you don't deserve? Yet, Joseph chose to forgive. Looking back, God who knew his heart granted that wherever they put him, (Joseph), God was with him and prospered him.

> 16 So they sent messengers to Joseph, saying, "Before your father died he commanded, saying, 17 'Thus you shall say to Joseph: "I beg you, please forgive the trespass of your brothers and their sin; for they did evil to you." Now, please, forgive the trespass of the servants of the God of your father." And Joseph wept when they spoke to him. 18 Then his brothers also went and fell down before his face, and they said, "Behold, we are your servants." 19 Joseph said to them, "Do not be afraid, for am I in the place of God? 20 But as for you, you meant evil against me; but God meant it for good, in order to bring it about as it is this day, to save many people alive. 21 Now

therefore, do not be afraid; I will provide for you and your little ones." And he comforted them and spoke kindly to them. Genesis 50:16–21.

Prayer points:

No matter the challenges, Lord Almighty, please fast-track me to my moments of glory in the name of Jesus Christ

Regardless of the activities of my antagonists, Lord Almighty, fast-track me to my moments of miracles in the name of Jesus Christ

Almighty Father, because of your mercy, direct me to my place of turnaround in the name of Jesus Christ

God of grace, please take me to my place of destiny-fulfilment in the name of Jesus Christ

How were all these processed and handled by a young man who at best started the journey at the age of seventeen but now is thirty years old? Who and what helped Joseph to cope? Was there pressure, any noticeable mental health and psychological issues, or likely emotional damage while the episode lasted? Perhaps we will never know. Obviously, before they reconciled, the entire situation was so deplorable that his half-brothers dishonestly made their father (Jacob) believed that Joseph was dead, Genesis 37:31–35, which was not true, but the deception went on for some years before it was detected during the famine that occurred, Genesis 45:1–4.

> 31 So they took Joseph's tunic, killed a kid of the goats, and dipped the tunic in the blood. 32 Then they sent the tunic of many colours, and they brought it to their father and said,

"We have found this. Do you know whether it is your son's tunic or not?"33 And he recognized it and said, "It is my son's tunic. A wild beast has devoured him. Without doubt Joseph is torn to pieces." 34 Then Jacob tore his clothes, put sackcloth on his waist, and mourned for his son many days. 35 And all his sons and all his daughters arose to comfort him; but he refused to be comforted, and he said, "For I shall go down into the grave to my son in mourning." Thus his father wept for him. Genesis 37:31–35.

How long have you faced your challenges for? Have you lost hope? Have people been horrible or deceptive towards you? Realise that God will do what He promised, like it happened in Genesis 21:1-2 and every day is a step closer to your miracles.

And the LORD visited Sarah as He had said, and the LORD did for Sarah as He had spoken. 2 For Sarah conceived and bore Abraham a son in his old age, at the set time of which God had spoken to him. Genesis 21:1-2

Then Joseph could not restrain himself before all those who stood by him, and he cried out, "Make everyone go out from me!" So no one stood with him while Joseph made himself known to his brothers. 2 And he wept aloud, and the Egyptians and the house of Pharaoh heard it. 3 Then Joseph said to his brothers, "I am Joseph; does my father still live?" But his brothers could not answer him, for they were dismayed in his presence. 4 And Joseph said to his brothers, "Please come near to me." So they came near. Then he said: "I am Joseph your brother, whom you sold into Egypt. Genesis 45:1–4.

It shall be tears of joy for you from today as it turned out for Joseph in Genesis 45:1-4. Whatever that made you cry in the past, will reverse and give you joy, peace, testimony, healing and miracles in the name of Jesus Christ. In hindsight, could being born into a polygamous home be the cause of Joseph's trouble? Realistically, it would be wrong to lay the entire blame on a polygamous marriage or relationship because during that time, it was acceptable to marry more than one wife and still have some concubines. It is worth remembering that they practised agrarian economy at the time, so they needed a large population to help in their farms. Talking about animosity, vulnerability, sibling rivalry, harassment and physical abuse as mentioned earlier, how likely could any of the experience affect Joseph's chance to becoming a world-class leader? Being in his shoes, would you have thought about offering them forgiveness even when you became a top-class leader in the whole world? What does it really mean to be a Joseph?

Paying the price – Joseph

For Joseph to be the person God has ordained for him to be, he had to leave the comfort of his family home, be disengaged from his family, against his will and intention and unprepared, to go to Egypt. Joseph was sold as a slave when he went there. The interesting little parallel here is that, Joseph's great grand-father (Abraham) unlike Joseph who was sold to slavery to Egypt, was instructed to leave his kith and kindred to a land which God would show him, Genesis 12:1. Does that mean relocation is one of the tools God uses for the fulfilment of destiny assignments? Can we remember that it was this same Egypt that Isaac wanted to go to and God forbade him? Genesis 26:1–2.

> Now the LORD had said to Abram: "Get out of your country, From your family and from your father's house, To a land that I will show you. Genesis 12:1.

> There was a famine in the land, besides the first famine that was in the days of Abraham. And Isaac went to Abimelech king of the Philistines, in Gerar. 2 Then the LORD appeared to him and said: "Do not go down to Egypt; live in the land of which I shall tell you. Genesis 26:1-2.

In today's world many would think it was foolhardy or reckless to embark on a journey which the individual lacks full details, but with God directing the affairs, His plans would definitely be worth it. Did Joseph really have a choice in whatever that was happening? Was his permission sought, or required in this matter? Would his agreement to the situation, or disagreement have changed things? Anyway Joseph finally arrived in Egypt, Genesis 39:1. Everything rolled out like a carpet which an individual must walk on, or as a script which an actor was bound to act the play. And the lot fell on Joseph the second to the last born of Jacob.

> Now Joseph had been taken down to Egypt. And Potiphar, an officer of Pharaoh, captain of the guard, an Egyptian, bought him from the Ishmaelites who had taken him down there. Genesis 39:1.

He is a slave now!

It appears like a sudden shock but no one knows how Joseph felt in his new environment or role, which can best be described as a dignified slave. Does anybody care about him now? Know his whereabouts? What does the future hold for the dreamer whom God has revealed he was going to be a great man? How best can he be described in his new found job? Can there ever be a job satisfaction while on this job? Any prospect of becoming a great person, or expect promotion after some time? It all looks unpromising, but to be 'the Joseph,' it meant that he was bound to be at his best, work hard, guard himself against temptation, avoid sinful life and lifestyle, and let God complete the rest. Unfortunately, soon danger was looming and Joseph needed to be sober and vigilant because the adversary was not only lurking around, but seeking to destroy him and his destiny. To be 'the Joseph' meant that, he had to resist the devil! 1 Peter 5:8-9. For the benefit of the doubt, the agent the devil prepared for the attack that was to be launched was Potiphar's wife, Genesis 39:10–12.

> 8 Be sober, be vigilant; because your adversary the devil walks about like a roaring lion, seeking whom he may devour. 9 Resist him, steadfast in the **faith,** knowing that the same sufferings are experienced by your brotherhood in the world. 1 Peter 5:8–9.

The die is cast! Genesis 39:10–12

Joseph must be growing in self confidence in his new found employment at Potiphar's house. It can be remembered that in the past he went through some betrayal, conspiracy, pain and rejection, but he believed that God had some plans for him. Will these thoughts be helpful for his survival at any point in his life? What does destiny hold for him up to this point, and can his future be any better?

> 10 So it was, as she spoke to Joseph day by day, that he did not heed her, to lie with her *or* to be with her. 11 But it happened about this time, when Joseph went into the house to do his work, and none of the men of the house *was* inside, 12 that she caught him by his garment, saying, "Lie with me." But he left his garment in her hand, and fled and ran outside. Genesis 39:10–12.

Disowned and Imprisonment

Joseph who was once disowned by his blood brothers and eventually sold into slavery will be disowned again and would be sent to prison by his favoured master, Genesis 39:19-20.

> 19 So it was, when his master heard the words which his wife spoke to him, saying, "Your servant did to me after this manner," that his anger was aroused. 20 Then Joseph's master took him and put him into the prison, a place where the king's prisoners *were* confined. And he was there in the prison. Genesis 39:19-20.

Will God who delivered Joseph when he was thrown into a dry well do it again? Would that past memory trigger any mental health challenge? In life people go through all kinds of experience, will the memory ever allow Joseph to forgive his brothers now that he is imprisoned? Of course he did as we shall be find out later.

The Divine Instrument – Joseph

Earlier, it is recorded how his master trusted him and gave him the liberty to do anything necessary for the house to run properly. The next place for Joseph as he would discover shortly, is the prison. A prison is supposed to a place for reform and correction, but what do we expect to be going on in Joseph's mind? Does that bear any semblance with God's promises for him? Does he deserve this imprisonment especially when proper investigation was not conducted with a proven evidence to show that a crime has been duly committed? The conclusion of the matter at this point is that, Joseph is jailed or sentenced to prison for a time period. However, as a slave and a foreigner, he had no legal rights at all, no hope for when he would be released after serving his jail sentence, or be entitled to parole. It is entirely in God's hands now.

As a matter of fact, the alleged crime attracted an immediate beheading but how he was spared can be attributed to God who knew the truth and was ready to preserve this individual who is a type of saviour, or the pre-incarnate of Christ. As recorded, Joseph went through some suffering, Psalm 105:17-24, they hurt his feet with fetters and placed his neck in an iron collar during his imprisonment. Nevertheless, he was a divine instrument who was meant to be in Egypt when he did. Being the case, God cannot be queried regarding the method He chose to use, or why He allowed such incident to happen. It should be understood that God is sovereign and He chooses to do things the way He wants them to be done.

> He sent a man before them – Joseph – *who* was sold as a slave. 18 They hurt his feet with fetters, He was laid in irons. 19 Until the time that his word came to pass, The word of the LORD tested him. 20 The king sent and released him, The ruler of the people let him go free. 21 He made him lord of his house, And ruler of all his possessions, 22 To bind his princes at his pleasure, And teach his elders wisdom. 23 Israel also came into Egypt, And Jacob dwelt in the land of Ham. 24 He increased His people greatly, And made them stronger than their enemies. Psalm 105:17–24.

SPIRITUAL CHECK-UP

My soul is among lions; I lie among the sons of men Who are set on fire, Whose teeth are spears and arrows, And their tongue a sharp sword. Psalm 57:4.

To what extent do you want to trust people if you were conspired against like Joseph, disowned, rejected, got into trouble with a seductive woman and jailed for a crime you didn't commit?

Task:

Carefully meditate and prayerfully compile a list about where you are hurting, then ask for God's help so you can forgive and forget.

....
....
....
....
....
....
....
....
....
....
....

CHAPTER NINE

BEST PRACTICE

There are many opinions in regards to forgiveness as a topic, and most important of all only a few people really agree that no matter what happens, people should forgive and forget exactly as God forgave humans wholly out of love. Of a truth, this is God's standard and if anyone is looking for the best practice that is it. Can you imagine the Saviour of the world being terribly beaten, bled badly, spat on, disgraced and ridiculed publicly, forced to carry a heavy Cross for a long distance, and finally nailed on the Cross to die? An individual was so unhelpful in that instead of water he gave sour wine to Jesus when the latter was dehydrated on the Cross, thirsty and was about to die. Yet, in the end He was begging God to forgive the perpetrators Luke 23:33–35, and by wider implication for all people.

> 33 And when they had come to the place called Calvary, there they crucified Him, and the criminals, one on the right hand and the other on the left. 34 Then Jesus said, "Father, forgive them, for they do not know what they do." And they divided His garments and cast lots. 35 And the people stood looking on. But even the rulers with them sneered, saying, "He saved others; let Him save Himself if He is the Christ, the chosen of God." Luke 23:33–35.

For the benefit of the doubt, Calvary (skull in Latin), was the place of execution or death, there Jesus was placed in-between two criminals having been accused, judged, mocked and sentenced to death for the crime He didn't commit. It was unimaginable to see Jesus numbered among criminals having gone around healing the sick, raising the dead, and doing all good things. Up to now, with infinite love and mercy He cried on the Cross to the Father for humanity to be forgiven.[42]

Going forward, there is so much forgiveness to be offered to people around the various network of relationships every person belong to in society. As much as depending on individuals, there is no way any of us can escape it, people will offend you, some may be close friends, family members, Church members, School mates, colleagues from workplace, distant relations or complete strangers. As long as we remain humans, there is no guarantee that we won't offend people, or people won't offend us. I have some questions to refresh our minds.

Question Time — Six questions at a glance

1. What do you do if you were the one who offended another person?

2. What should be the best way to protect oneself throughout one's lifetime such that nobody succeeds in offending you?

3. Can we ever find a person who can provide detailed guidelines which can help him or her to navigate around issues such that no matter how many times people try to hurt them, they won't succeed?

4. Is there a person in life who has not wronged or offended someone before, apart from Jesus Christ?

---

[42] William MacDonald, (Art Farstad, ed.,), *Believer's Bible Commentary*, London: Thomas Nelson Publishers, 1989, p. 1455

5. What is the best practice, or a possible method through which nobody will be able to hurt you?

6. What can make you remain unforgiving and is the issue new under the sun?

David the son of Jesse

Fortunately, apart from Jesus' exemplary way in which He begged God while nailed and agonising on the Cross for forgiveness for those who condemned Him, we can find another biblical individual who demonstrated that he would be forgiving almost to a fault. David who was known for his moral weakness as a result of what happened between him and Bathsheba, 2 Samuel 11:2-5, was able to truly forgive some people as we shall soon see.

> 2 Then it happened one evening that David arose from his bed and walked on the roof of the king's house. And from the roof he saw a woman bathing, and the woman was very beautiful to behold. 3 So David sent and inquired about the woman. And someone said, "Is this not Bathsheba, the daughter of Eliam, the wife of Uriah the Hittite?" 4 Then David sent messengers, and took her; and she came to him, and he lay with her, for she was cleansed from her impurity; and she returned to her house. 5 And the woman conceived; so she sent and told David, and said, "I am with child." 2 Samuel 11:2-5.

Interestingly, one of the lessons here is that, everyone should know that times of idleness can be times of the greatest temptation. This same David who was caught in an act of moral lapse became the father of King Solomon. The latter was attributed as having wide knowledge of many subjects, for he spoke about three thousand proverbs, produced one thousand and five songs, spoke about trees, animals, birds and other creeping things, 1 Kings 4:32–33. What a gift!

> 32 He spoke three thousand proverbs, and his songs were one thousand and five. 33 Also he spoke of trees, from the cedar tree of Lebanon even to the hyssop that springs out of the wall; he spoke also of animals, of birds, of creeping things, and of fish. 1 Kings 4:32–33.

Irrespective of the moral weakness, God had said David was the man after His own heart, **1 Samuel 13:14**. What does that imply? God had known that David would prove himself as a true representative of God and would work dependently with Him fully in all his dealings, therefore, it should not be surprising that God made that remark.

> 14 But now your kingdom shall not continue. The LORD has sought for Himself a man after His own heart, and the LORD has commanded him to be commander over His people, because you have not kept what the LORD commanded you. 1 Samuel 13:14.

Some may be wondering what criteria God had used in arriving at this decision but He knows best. Importantly, people may like to know how good David's sense of justice was, and how understanding was he to have warranted such commendation? Was David great at forgiving other people? The truth is, we have so much to learn from David regarding forgiveness, for instance, he forgave Absalom when he was appealed to, 2 Samuel 14:21. Let us remember how Absalom was responsible for the death of Amnon his half-brother who raped Tamar his sister, 2 Samuel 13:37–39. Not only that, about forty years later Absalom revolted against his father David, 2 Samuel 15:7.

21 And the king said to Joab, "All right, I have granted this thing. Go therefore, bring back the young man Absalom." 2 Samuel 14:21.

37 But Absalom fled and went to Talmai the son of Ammihud, king of Geshur. And *David* mourned for his son every day. 38 So Absalom fled and went to Geshur, and was there three years. 39 And King David longed to go to Absalom. For he had been comforted concerning Amnon, because he was dead. 2 Samuel 13:37–39.

7 Now it came to pass after forty years that Absalom said to the king, "Please, let me go to Hebron and pay the vow which I made to the LORD. 8 For your servant took a vow while I dwelt at Geshur in Syria, saying, 'If the LORD indeed brings me back to Jerusalem, then I will serve the LORD.' 2 Samuel 15:7.

Absalom's Treason

Further, after forgiving Absalom for the murder case, it is surprising but true that this unrepentant Absalom with the help of some of the tribes of Israel conspired and dethroned David, 2 Samuel 15:10–14. Could it be that Absalom tried to use Hebron his place of birth to launch an attack against his father's throne? Or if the people of Hebron were unhappy that David had moved his capital from Hebron to Jerusalem, should Absalom use them for his over ambitious political career in return for the complete pardon he had received? How would you have reacted against someone called your son who concealed in his heart the desire to usurp the throne when you are still active, healthy, fit and not about to die? Regardless, David continued to wish him well even though Absalom formed his new government.

> 10 Then Absalom sent spies throughout all the tribes of Israel, saying, "As soon as you hear the sound of the trumpet, then you shall say, 'Absalom reigns in Hebron!'" 11 And with Absalom went two hundred men invited from Jerusalem, and they went along innocently and did not know anything. 12 Then Absalom sent for Ahithophel the Gilonite, David's counsellor, from his city – from Giloh – while he offered sacrifices. And the conspiracy grew strong, for the people with Absalom continually increased in number. 13 Now a messenger came to David, saying, "The hearts of the men of Israel are with Absalom." 14 So David said to all his servants who *were* with him at Jerusalem, "Arise, and let us flee, or we shall not escape from Absalom. Make haste to depart, lest he overtake us suddenly and bring disaster upon us, and strike the city with the edge of the sword." 2 Samuel 15:10–14.

As a result of Absalom's insurrection David fled Jerusalem with some of his followers but he was never bitter despite the exile been unwarranted, instead he submitted meekly to God's will and used the time to compose Psalm 3 where he emphasised his trust in the Lord.[43]

Notwithstanding, when the time came for David's army to quash the rebellion, he appealed for Absalom's life be spared, 2 Samuel 18:5, unfortunately Absalom died in the battle, 2 Samuel 18:14–15. As we read later, David never rejoiced at the death of Absalom who revolted against him and his government, rather it grieved his heart on hearing the news about Absalom's death and he lamented pathetically, 2 Samuel 18:33. Some people naturally were jubilant at

---

[43] William MacDonald, (Editor Art Farstad), *Believer's Bible Commentary,* London: Thomas Nelson Publishers, 1995, p. 339

hearing that their 'enemy' is dead, but not David, as it can be deduced from his deep mourning for his son, also it is obvious that he forgave his son despite the two atrocities Absalom committed.

> 5 Now the king had commanded Joab, Abishai, and Ittai, saying, "Deal gently for my sake with the young man Absalom." And all the people heard when the king gave all the captains orders concerning Absalom. 2 Samuel 18:5.

> 14 Then Joab said, "I cannot linger with you." And he took three spears in his hand and thrust them through Absalom's heart, while he was still alive in the midst of the terebinth tree. 15 And ten young men who bore Joab's armour surrounded Absalom, and struck and killed him. 2 Samuel 18:14–15.

> 33 Then the king was deeply moved, and went up to the chamber over the gate, and wept. And as he went, he said thus: "O my son Absalom – my son, my son Absalom – if only I had died in your place! O Absalom my son, my son!" 2 Samuel 18:33.

Persecution and death threat – King Saul

Further, if it is not clear enough about how Absalom was forgiven, we can be reminded about David's experience from the time he stepped into the palace and began to sing so that the depressive spirit that used to trouble King Saul would depart from the him, 1 Samuel 16:23.

> And so it was, whenever the spirit from God was upon Saul, that David would take a harp and play it with his hand. Then Saul would become refreshed and well, and the distressing spirit would depart from him. 1 Samuel 16:23.

David's victory at the battlefield made Saul to be extremely jealous, he demoted David militarily from being Saul's armour bearer to captain over a thousand, 1 Samuel 18:13. For all David's services to Saul personally and to his government, what did Saul try to give as a reward to David? Simply, he attempted to kill David twice in one day, 1 Samuel 18:10–11.

> 10 And it happened on the next day that the distressing spirit from God came upon Saul, and he prophesied inside the house. So David played music with his hand, as at other times; but there was a spear in Saul's hand. 11 And Saul cast the spear, for he said, "I will pin David to the wall!" But David escaped his presence twice. 1 Samuel 18:10–11.

However, that was not the only occasion he attempted on David's life. Other instances include luring David to become the King's in-law thereby demanding an extraordinary dowry which was a death trap. To be precise, King Saul demanded one hundred foreskins of the Philistines which Saul had thought would lead to David's death on the battlefield and make it appear like the latter died in a military service, 1 Samuel 18:25.

> Then Saul said, "Thus you shall say to David: 'The king does not desire any dowry but one hundred foreskins of the Philistines, to take vengeance on the king's enemies.'" But Saul thought to make David fall by the hand of the Philistines. 1 Samuel 18:25.

Again with the help of God, David continued to excel militarily despite Saul's hatred for him, and he paid twice the demanded dowry, yet, Saul continually persecuted David and saw him as his chief enemy, 1 Samuel 18:29.

> And Saul was still more afraid of David. So Saul became David's enemy continually. 1 Samuel 18:29.

The question is, how do you please someone who constantly sees you as a threat and wished you were dead and you don't even think evil towards the individual? Some of the instances discussed show the relationship between Saul and David to be overly suspicious of who David was not, 1 Samuel 19:1, 10-12.

> Now Saul spoke to Jonathan his son and to all his servants that they should kill David; but Jonathan, Saul's son, delighted greatly in David. 1 Samuel 19:1.

> 10 Then Saul sought to pin David to the wall with the spear, but he slipped away from Saul's presence; and he drove the spear into the wall. So David fled and escaped that night. 11 Saul also sent messengers to David's house to watch him and to kill him in the morning. And Michal, David's wife, told him, saying, "If you do not save your life tonight, tomorrow you will be killed." 12 So Michal let David down through a window. And he went and fled and escaped. 1 Samuel 19:10–12.

Again, King Saul took three thousand special military personnel and went into the desert to kill David, 1 Samuel 24:2.

> Then Saul took three thousand chosen men from all Israel, and went to seek David and his men on the Rocks of the Wild Goats. I Samuel 24:2.

Incidentally, there was a particular cave in the desert where David was hiding, but Saul entered there to ease himself and was unaware of David's presence there at the time. What can prevent David from killing Saul now? Definitely, the opportunity was there for David to kill king Saul, but he only cut off the tip of Saul's material as evidence, and allowed the latter to leave the cave alive, 1 Samuel 24:4. In David's position today, would you have spared your 'enemy'? Somebody ruthlessly hunting for your life? But David did.

> 4 Then the men of David said to him, "This is the day of which the LORD said to you, 'Behold, I will deliver your enemy into your hand that you may do to him as it seems good to you.'" And David arose and secretly cut off a corner of Saul's robe. 1 Samuel 24:4.

Soon after, David called Saul's attention to what had happened, 1 Samuel 24:9-11, and how he (David) chose not to kill Saul. David chose to be kind to the one who was mercilessly hunting for his life. Do you think it is easy to forgive? It can be difficult for a natural man but note that, one of the key things to understand is that those who want to forgive their fellows never think about how to avenge themselves.

> 9 And David said to Saul: "Why do you listen to the words of men who say, 'Indeed David seeks your harm'? 10 Look, this day your eyes have seen that the LORD delivered you today into my hand in the cave, and someone urged me to kill you. But my eye spared you, and I said, 'I will not stretch out my hand against my lord, for he is the LORD's anointed.' 11 Moreover, my father, see! Yes, see the corner of your robe in my hand! For in that I cut off the corner of your robe, and did not kill you, know and see that there is neither evil nor rebellion in my hand, and I have not sinned against you. Yet you hunt my life to take it. 1 Samuel 24:9–11.

King Saul was the erratic type in that he would speak nicely but his actions did not corroborate his words, which makes one to wonder when he would stop persecuting David. It is extraordinarily wonderful to see David trustingly calm in the face of all this adversity. The difference between the two of them is remarkable. Surprisingly, Saul admitted David was more righteous than himself, 1 Samuel 24:17, 21–22.

> 17 Then he said to David: "You are more righteous than I; for you have rewarded me with good, whereas I have rewarded you with evil. 21 Therefore swear now to me by the LORD that you will not cut off my descendants after me, and that you will not destroy my name from my father's house." ... 22 So David swore to Saul. And Saul went home, but David and his men went up to the stronghold. 1 Samuel 24:17, 21–22.

For David sparing Saul's life in all the above instances, the expectation should be for Saul to return to his palace and consider the matter closed and leave David alone. Shockingly, Saul returned to seek David's life again, 1 Samuel 26:2, but David spared his life once more, and returned the items they took away while Saul was sleeping, 1 Samuel 26:11, 22–23.

> 2 Then Saul arose and went down to the Wilderness of Ziph, having three thousand chosen men of Israel with him, to seek David in the Wilderness of Ziph. 1 Samuel 26:2.

> 11 The LORD forbid that I should stretch out my hand against the LORD's anointed. But please, take now the spear and the jug of water that are by his head, and let us go ... 22 And David answered and said, "Here is the king's spear. Let one of the young men come over and get it. 23 May the LORD repay every man for his righteousness

and his faithfulness; for the LORD delivered you into my hand today, but I would not stretch out my hand against the LORD's anointed. 1 Samuel 26:11, 22–23.

To some people, it might be appropriate to imagine or take David's open-heartedness for stupidity, however, if there were special awards for those who can forgive unconditionally, David deserves one for being this patient, tolerant and forgiving towards king Saul. Anybody can conclude that such an individual like Saul who persecuted David severally with the intention to kill him must not be forgiven, they can be right in their own judgment, but David was not the type to tolerate lack of forgiveness. He was not ready to kill Saul not even under the pretence that he acted in self-defence. He did exactly what God wants all His children to do. Forgive.

Abigail and Nabal, then Shimei

It goes beyond magnanimity what David did regarding King Saul, and if anyone thinks because Saul happened to be a king that was why David tolerated him that much, and treated Saul differently, they better think twice because it was not really so. Indeed he forgave Nabal and Shimei as well. In a nutshell, he suggests the best practice to be adopted as we navigate our journey on earth called life, is to learn to be forgiving. Again, in regards to David, should it be a case of, to whom much is forgiven, much forgiveness is expected? Of course it looks like it especially, his relationship with Bathsheba and what he did to her husband Uriah are constant reminders. However, for the benefit of the doubt, one finds that by proxy Nabal was forgiven when Abigail pleaded on his behalf, 1 Samuel 25:21–28, 32–35, so also an individual called Shimei, 2 Samuel 16:7-14, they were completely forgiven in their individual capacity.

Nabal – Forgiven by proxy

He was a farmer whose business flourished during that time but lacked sensitivity towards the needs of others, his sense of gratitude regarding those who helped in the past either was shallow, or non-existent, yet he was in a position to help, but did not care. Worse of all, it is inhuman to be selfish when an occasion demands that goodwill should be shared, in particular when he was having a feast to mark a successful business year in modern day terminology. Nabal from the biblical account would not have any of the above even though he was wealthy and capable of helping. When such a person offends an individual, it can be difficult for the other person or party to feel obligated to forgive them, or the person might be unwilling to forgive completely.

> 21 Now David had said, "Surely in vain I have protected all that this fellow has in the wilderness, so that nothing was missed of all that belongs to him. And he has repaid me evil for good. 22 May God do so, and more also, to the enemies of David, if I leave one male of all who belong to him by morning light." 23 Now when Abigail saw David, she dismounted quickly from the donkey, fell on her face before David, and bowed down to the ground. 24 So she fell at his feet and said: "On me, my lord, on me let this iniquity be! And please let your maidservant speak in your ears, and hear the words of your maidservant. 25 Please, let not my lord regard this scoundrel Nabal. For as his name is, so is he: Nabal is his name, and folly is with him! But I, your maidservant, did not see the young men of my lord whom you sent. 26 Now therefore, my lord, as the LORD lives and as your soul lives, since the LORD has held you back from coming to bloodshed and from avenging yourself with your own hand, now then, let your enemies and those who seek harm for my lord be as Nabal. 27 And now this

present which your maidservant has brought to my lord, let it be given to the young men who follow my lord. 28 Please forgive the trespass of your maidservant. For the LORD will certainly make for my lord an enduring house, because my lord fights the battles of the LORD, and evil is not found in you throughout your days. 1 Samuel 25:21-28.

However, as it happened, Abigail his more discerning wife, unknown to Nabal acted swiftly and wisely to rectify the situation. It was her involvement that resulted to the forgiveness and avoidance of execution that David and his crew had intended against Nabal's family, 1 Samuel 25:32-35.

32 Then David said to Abigail: "Blessed is the LORD God of Israel, who sent you this day to meet me! 33 And blessed is your advice and blessed are you, because you have kept me this day from coming to bloodshed and from avenging myself with my own hand. 34 For indeed, as the LORD God of Israel lives, who has kept me back from hurting you, unless you had hurried and come to meet me, surely by morning light no males would have been left to Nabal!" 35 So David received from her hand what she had brought him, and said to her, "Go up in peace to your house. See, I have heeded your voice and respected your person." 1 Samuel 25:32-35.

As it turned out, the forgiveness benefited all the parties who were involved in this impasse, in that bloodshed was avoided at Nabal's family home, Abigail who halted the oncoming attack earns the respect she deserves, and David and his men returned to their station with lots of foodstuff. This shows how good, honourable and beneficial forgiving those who offend you can be. Also, everybody wins and each person or people group have something to celebrate for.

Shimei

He was a descendant of King Saul and as a Benjamite, he felt obligated to use the opportunity of Absalom's revolt to voice out his hatred for David whom he thought was an enemy of King Saul. His behaviour towards David was horrible and provocative. Furthermore, Shimei was rude, insulting and cursed David during his predicament, 2 Samuel 16:7–14.

> 7 Also Shimei said thus when he cursed: "Come out! Come out! You bloodthirsty man, you rogue! 8 The LORD has brought upon you all the blood of the house of Saul, in whose place you have reigned; and the LORD has delivered the kingdom into the hand of Absalom your son. So now you are caught in your own evil, because you are a bloodthirsty man!" 9 Then Abishai the son of Zeruiah said to the king, "Why should this dead dog curse my lord the king? Please, let me go over and take off his head!" 10 But the king said, "What have I to do with you, you sons of Zeruiah? So let him curse, because the LORD has said to him, 'Curse David.' Who then shall say, 'Why have you done so?' " 11 And David said to Abishai and all his servants, "See how my son who came from my own body seeks my life. How much more now may this Benjamite? Let him alone, and let him curse; for so the LORD has ordered him. 12 It may be that the LORD will look on my affliction, and that the LORD will repay me with good for his cursing this day." 13 And as David and his men went along the road, Shimei went along the hillside opposite him and cursed as he went, threw stones at him and kicked up dust. 14 Now the king and all the people who were with him became weary; so they refreshed themselves there. 2 Samuel 16:7–14.

Although, David had the ability to kill Shimei straightaway, he decided to spare his life even when one of his officers requested his permission, he did not approve. Further, his ability to control himself in the face of provocation was commendable and really makes him to be a genuine forgiver, and what he did that time, reminds us that vengeance indeed belongs to God and that was David's preferred choice. In addition, David might be on his way to exile but had not lost his sense of direction, rather he shows he was in control of his emotions and still in charge of all the events going on around him. As exemplary as David's behaviour was, it is important to realise that people's excessive hostility like Shimei displayed, can move God to show mercy on the insulted person.

It is all about forgiveness and David sends this message clearer through his restraint and a balanced sense of judgment by refusing permission for one of his officers when he wanted to kill Shimei because of his indecent behaviour. There are many people who sometimes take the wrong side in life without knowing, Shimei we should understand, most likely didn't know how much we know about what transpired in the palace between David and Saul, the marriage between Michal and David which was a death trap, and the eventual harassment and persecution in the wilderness with three thousand special military troops of Saul looking for one man to kill.

Forgiveness cannot make sense

Forgiveness cannot make sense if we fail to see it in God's truly way (Biblical). Jesus is the foundation for forgiveness and it must be understood that forgiveness is hard, but possible. This has been proved by examples previously provided from the preceding pages in this book. To recall, the only petition in Our Lord's Prayer as written in Matthew 6:14-15, that has a condition attached to it is forgiveness (Greek: aphesin*[44]). Forgiveness should never be taken for granted. As astutely expressed by an eminent theologian, forgiveness began in the heart of God and extended to the heart of every person, anyone who refuses to forgive burns the bridge over which he or she must cross to receive their own forgiveness.[45] Let me add this, so long as you believe you are a child of God, created in His image and after His likeness, then you are obligated to forgive as God would forgive— you are not allowed to burn the bridge over which you must cross to receive your own forgiveness. Needless to say, forgive and you will be forgiven by God. Don't forgive and you won't be forgiven, period!

In one of the most gruesome occurrence in this modern day, we read Dawn Smith Jordan's story about her seventeen year old sister called Sheerie. The latter was abducted as she walked from her car to the mailbox and was not discovered until five days later. Sheerie who was kidnapped, raped and killed was allowed to write her last letter to her family by the kidnapper, rapist and murderer. As was narrated, Sheerie wrote what she called "my last will and testament" and she said, "I love you all so much. Please don't let this ruin your lives. Keep living one day at a time for Jesus. Don't worry about me because I know I'm going to be with my Father." And she was gone forever! Can you believe that? That was somebody's daughter, sister, friend, supposedly wife, mother, aunty, etc., but killed untimely.

---

[44] This Greek word (Aphesin) literally means action taken that leads to freedom and reconciliation
[45] Clinton L. Ryan, *European Theological Seminary*, Hockley, Birmingham: Majesty Print, 2002, p. 9

However, as if it was not enough losing Sheerie, the kidnapper, rapist and murderer kept phoning the family numerously for days, describing the horrible details about how Sheerie was murdered. Would you ever want to do anything with this person, or forgive this kidnapper, rapist and murderer called Mr Bell if you came across him? But a few years later, he became a Christian and wrote to late Sheerie's family begging for forgiveness. It was difficult but not impossible. As Dawn (late Sheerie's sister) struggled, she remembered God's word in Ephesians 4:32 and forgave Mr Bell— telling Mr Bell that she (Dawn) could forgive because she too had received God's grace in her life.[46]

> 32 And be kind to one another, broken-hearted, forgiving one another, even as God in Christ forgave you. Ephesians 4:32

It might not make human sense but that is what God requires from us— to take action that would produce freedom and reconciliation like Dawn, Colossians 3:12-13.

> 12 Therefore, as the elect of God, holy and beloved, put on tender mercies, kindness, humility, meekness, longsuffering; 13 bearing with one another, and forgiving one another, if anyone has a complaint against another; even as Christ forgave you, so you also must do. Colossians 3:12-13

Can we really forget when we forgive?

As we forgive and try to forget, there is need to look for lasting healing but note that our memories will play up—this should not be allowed to confuse us, cause unnecessary guilt

---

[46] Robert Jeffress, *When Forgiveness Doesn't Make Sense*, Colorado Springs, Colorado: Waterbrook Press, 2000, pp. 19-20

or bitterness which can lead us to be defiled or sin against God, Hebrews 12:15.

> 15 looking carefully lest anyone fall short of the grace of God; lest any root of bitterness springing up cause trouble, and by this many become defiled. Hebrews 12:15

Forgetting depends on our minds there is no doubt about it, but we have to try and allow the spirit to prevail over the flesh like Dawn did in the above story. Of course many times the spirit will be willing whereas the flesh can be weak. Don't get me wrong, some school of thought believe that the aspect of 'forgetting' after you have forgiven would be impossible. True, because human brain has capacity to store so much, but whatever you can remember about an incident you forgave, or have forgiven, do not allow it to bring back rage, bitterness or vengeance. Make up your mind to forgive and forget. What to do?

Commit into your memory, memorise or meditate constantly some of the following Bible passages especially as you try to forgive and forget, Isaiah 44:22; Matthew 6:12-15; 18:33-35; Ephesians 4:31-32; Colossians 3:12-13; Philippians 4:8.

Hand over everything to God and prayerfully draw strength from Him one day at a time. Trust Him.

Apart from the above Bible passages, take this graphic image from me, let the incident be like something you have thrown to the depth of an ocean and allow the "current" to sweep it away for you— imagine the "current" to be Holy Spirit doing the cleansing for you. Is that not better? Micah 7:19.

> He will again have compassion on us, And will subdue our iniquities. You will cast all our sins into the depths of the sea. Micah 7:19

Are you struggling within yourself that God has not forgiven you? Or you keep remembering your sins? Or what someone did to you? As suggested by a distinguished theologian, there are benefits in remembering, but it should be positive ones like he used Paul as a reference in 1 Timothy 1:12-16. Paul remembered everything about himself as any of us would— once a blasphemer, persecutor of the saints and so on.

> 12 And I thank Christ Jesus our Lord who has enabled me, because He counted me faithful, putting me into the ministry, 13 although I was formerly a blasphemer, a persecutor, and an insolent man; but I obtained mercy because I did it ignorantly in unbelief. 14 And the grace of our Lord was exceedingly abundant, with faith and love which are in Christ Jesus. 15 This is a faithful saying and worthy of all acceptance, that Christ Jesus came into the world to save sinners, of whom I am chief. 16 However, for this reason I obtained mercy, that in me first Jesus Christ might show all longsuffering, as a pattern to those who are going to believe on Him for everlasting life. 1 Timothy 1:12-16

Persistently, Paul's enemies never believed a persecutor would be used by God and he always had to contend with that fact thirty years after his conversion. Nevertheless, some of the benefits which happened when Paul recalled his past sins which can happen to any of us is that, firstly, the remembrance encouraged him to be grateful to God. For Paul the gracious act of forgiveness by God was too overwhelming. So we too can focus on the gracious act of God's forgiveness each time our memories play up. Secondly, though the memory lingered, but it destroyed Paul's pride hence, he calls himself 'chief of all sinners' whom God used, 1 Timothy 1:15. Let us remember God hates the proud but gives grace to the humble— James 4:6. For Paul, it turned out to be a blessing in disguise.

> This is a faithful saying and worthy of all acceptance, that Christ Jesus came into the world to save sinners, of whom I am chief. 1 Timothy 1:15

Thirdly, while remembering the past sins like any of us who could have felt horrible, Paul saw himself as someone on whom God had showered grace. Like Dawn whose sister was kidnapped, raped and killed professed, she remembered that she received grace in her life and handed forgiveness to Mr Bell. We all can go ahead and try to do the same. As succinctly stated by a respectable theologian, it was as if Paul was saying, "Look at me, if God is capable of forgiving me, He can certainly forgive you."[47] Consequent upon that, as Christian believers we are bound to forgive, forget and do whatever that is noble, pure and of good report like Dawn did, Philippians 4:8.

> Finally, brethren, whatever things are true, whatever things are noble, whatever things are just, whatever things are pure, whatever things are lovely, whatever things are of good report, if there is any virtue and if there is anything praiseworthy—meditate on these things. Philippians 4:8

There is no need to wait any longer, except to go ahead and be a forgiveness-practitioner. Simply, what are you waiting for?

---

[47] Robert Jeffress, *When Forgiveness Doesn't Make Sense*, Colorado Springs, Colorado: Waterbrook Press, 2000, pp. 134-135

SPIRITUAL CHECK-UP

Blessed is he whose transgression is forgiven, whose sin is covered. 2 Blessed is the man to whom the LORD does not impute iniquity, And in whose spirit there is no deceit. Psalm 32:1–2.

Who do you think you have wronged? Where did things go wrong and since when? Pray, meditate and ask God to show you and ask for grace to make amends.

....
....
....
....
....
....
....
....
....
....
....
....
....
....
....

CHAPTER TEN

WHAT ARE YOU WAITING FOR?

A particular couple offended me, apologised to me and I said okay, but deep down in my heart I resolved to relate to them from a distance from that day. Is that a failure to forgive? Well, this was a lady's opinion but when she died and found herself condemned to hell because of failure to forgive, she realised that she was wrong. It was almost too late for her to return to earth but Jesus spoke for her. What happened was that the persistent prayer of a woman she knew in their local Church but had died the previous year and now in heaven, made Jesus to show her mercy. The lady had already placed her left foot to pass through the gate of hell when Jesus intervened. Her testimony will follow shortly.

Failure to forgive can lead to detrimental consequences as the Bible says that anyone who fails to forgive makes it impossible for himself or herself to have fellowship with God, and will not be able to maintain one either, Matthew 6:15. This is huge to overlook if a person doesn't want to go to hell. Therefore, there is need for everyone to ensure that they adopt a lifestyle that allows for forgiveness.

> But if you do not forgive men their trespasses, neither will your Father forgive your trespasses. Matthew 6:15.

Importantly, any lack of forgiveness apart from other types of sins, constitutes unrighteousness which means that the individual will not inherit the kingdom of God unless they forgive while still alive, 1 Corinthians 6:9a.

Do you not know that the unrighteous will not inherit the kingdom of God?' 1 Corinthians 6:9a.

As Christian believers we are called to maintain peaceable co-existence among other humans, even in the face of persecution, to refrain from venting our anger at all times, tame our fears and frustration at each other when the situation becomes highly charged or tense. This is important so we can avoid regret later. The truth is, it is possible to remember some of the remarks afterwards and find it difficult to forgive, hence we have to forgive quickly, Hebrews 12:14.

14 Pursue peace with all people, and holiness, without which no one will see the Lord. Hebrews 12:14.

One of the uncontrollable factors but a fact of life is that, if people refuse to forgive now, nobody can guarantee a second chance tomorrow, because once they die, they have to face the consequences. For example, in an entirely different matter between two individuals, the request for a second chance was not granted. The story of the rich man and Lazarus comes to mind, Luke 16:19-31, although it was not about failure to forgive. The emphasis is based on the unlikelihood of a second chance being granted to someone who died to come back to life. It is recorded that the rich man wanted someone to be sent to his five brothers on earth to warn them to live righteously so that they won't end up in hell like himself. As good as the thoughts were, unfortunately the request was declined. Verdict: No second chance! The Bible states,

19 There was a certain rich man who was clothed in purple and fine linen and fared sumptuously every day. 20 But there was a certain beggar named Lazarus, full of sores, who was laid at his gate, 21 desiring to be fed with the crumbs which fell from the rich man's table. Moreover the dogs came and licked his sores. 22 So it was that the beggar died, and was carried by the angels to Abraham's bosom. The rich man also died and was buried. 23 And being in torments in Hades, he lifted up his eyes and saw Abraham afar off, and Lazarus in his bosom. 24 "Then he cried and said, 'Father Abraham, have mercy on me, and send Lazarus that he may dip the tip of his finger in water and cool my tongue; for I am tormented in this flame.' 25 But Abraham said, 'Son, remember that in your lifetime you received your good things, and likewise Lazarus evil things; but now he is comforted and you are tormented. 26 And besides all this, between us and you there is a great gulf fixed, so that those who want to pass from here to you cannot, nor can those from there pass to us.' 27 "Then he said, 'I beg you therefore, father, that you would send him to my father's house, 28 for I have five brothers, that he may testify to them, lest they also come to this place of torment.' 29 Abraham said to him, 'They have Moses and the prophets; let them hear them.' 30 And he said, 'No, father Abraham; but if one goes to them from the dead, they will repent.' 31 But he said to him, 'If they do not hear Moses and the prophets, neither will they be persuaded though one rise from the dead. Luke 16:19-31.

In the above narration, the rich man appealed for a second chance in heaven which was denied, how appreciative I guess he would have been! Further, the story does not relate to lack of pardon, not suggesting that being wealthy is sinful, rather it has to do with disregard for others – a beggar in the narrative, poor handling of stewardship of material things, lack of sensitivity to other people's needs, failure to show love to his fellow human which is tantamount to the fact that there was no God's love in him.

Additionally, the rich man's bodily pleasure and appetites or indulgence, were far more important to him than the kingdom. He was selfish and possibly stingy. The irony is that the Old Testament Jew believes that being wealthy is a sign of blessing from God. It is not true. In contrast, being poor does not qualify anyone to make heaven, rather the beggar entered the kingdom because he had trusted in God for the salvation of his soul, and it was not his beggarly condition that made him to be in heaven. For short, there is nothing to warrant a second chance being granted the rich man, or sending someone to go and warn his five brothers who were still alive.

However, Pastor Mrs Adejoke Oloko recounted her experience and was full of appreciation to God for her second chance. She is always ready to share her experience with God's children and some of her story has been shared on social media platforms. Her passion is to see that nobody goes to hell.

Testimony

A Guest At the Gate of Hell

(Narrated on Thursday 26/05/2022, produced with permission).

The opportunity for a second chance which was denied the rich man in the above story was granted me (Pastor

Mrs Adejoke Oloko) when I died and was allowed to return to this earth again. Heaven and Hell exist but heaven is the place all God's children should aspire to go to. Note this, from what I saw only a few people were walking towards the gate of heaven, whereas, those trooping towards the gate of hell were uncountable. Sadly they were chatting excitedly as they walked towards the gate of hell. How did I get there?

I had my baby through Caesarean Section and was discharged after about ten days to go home. But I had to return to the hospital on 16/09/2019, under twenty-four hours after being discharged because my tongue which started itching me on the left side, soon affected the right side and swelled uncontrollably until it was almost blocking my airway. I realised time was of essence and because my husband had travelled, I drove myself back to the hospital which was about a forty-five minutes journey. I alerted the hospital authorities about my condition before I took off. On arrival I was met by over twenty-five medical doctors and they immediately rushed me to the medical theatre.

I was conscious for a short period because my airway was almost totally blocked, my tongue had swollen badly and was sticking out. Suddenly, everything started to spin around in my eyes, including all the medical team trying to save my life. At first it was slowly and later it became very fast and scary and that was when I began to pray to God begging for forgiveness of my sins, and for me to make heaven, asking God to give my husband a new wife and let them look after my children. The last word I heard was, "1, 2, 3, push," then I had out of body experience. As I can recall, it was like pulling out an entity from a casing from my chest area then I saw my physical body lying on the bed and what the medical team was doing to it. I asked them, what are you doing? But there was no response from them? All I heard was, "Oh God we lost her." Then I said to them, No! I spoke to them again but they didn't respond. I tried touching them but my hand was entering their bodies, I became frantic, I ran to the monitor thinking it was faulty hence the funny noise coming from it, again my hand penetrated into the monitor, meanwhile I kept on saying, "I am not dead, I am not dead."

Yet, no one was able to hear me and I was getting frustrated at this period of time, then I saw some images like human figure lined up to my other side who confirmed to me the doctors cannot hear me. They requested me to follow them around, then I asked them who they were and they said they were wandering spirits. I refused their request and told them I didn't want to leave my body. I was able to see my human body still lying down on the medical bed. Not only that, but I was also able to see many things at once, all it required was, once I contemplate it in my mind, I will see it without moving an inch. Such was the experience I was going through when a gentleman in a three-piece suit came over to me and he wrapped his left arm around my right arm and whisked me away at a rocket speed, I didn't have control over the situation but could only cry and was saying, "I don't want to leave my body, I don't want to leave my body." The man did not care as we kept speeding off at an indescribable speed.

On looking beneath me, I saw the earth shrinking until it reduced to the size of an egg. I can remember how we passed through a dark tunnel, went past region-like places inhabited by dragon-like creatures, some with horns, tails covered with scales and so on. It was like journeying through the first heaven to the seventh then we came out of the tunnel. Shockingly, the man beat his chest three times and told me he was the spirit of death. Then I saw that he had a tail tucked inside his trousers, the tail had scales like a crocodile, and he dashed away at a full speed towards the direction which we came from.

Immediately after that, somebody said, welcome to me, in front of me while still dark and within that dark environment, an individual wearing a white attire, a male figure with glowing curly hair asked, "Do you know what you are doing here?" Strangely, a big fat book opened before me by itself, then I was told, "Your judgment commences now. "I was asked to read Psalm 24, as I got to where it says, "Lift up your head, O you gates!" Psalm 24:7, the entire environment vibrated and a very bright light shone from that direction, then I heard one of the grandmas who passed away in our local Church a year ago called Mama Don saying, "forgive her please because of thy song," and I was wondering who was Mama Don soliciting for? I saw flowers which looked like a sunflower were dancing to some music which was very great.

Also, a beam of light was shining on the Judgment panellists and no other person(s). They signalled judgement to start and that I should read Isaiah 54:17. This was their response to me regarding the scripture, the scripture is almost like a cliché among Christian believers, but the interpretation I was given in regards to the Bible passage is totally different from what most of us know, especially where it states, "and every tongue which rises against you in judgement you shall condemn," I was told it meant, "Your soul belongs to God, you have no right to offend the soul. Whoever does, the soul will judge the individual." Then they said to me, "Do you know the saints will judge the whole earth?" They made me to understand that, individuals are "the earth." The earth is the individual facing judgment. Next, I was asked to read

Matthew 6 where Our Lord's prayer is. When I got to where it says, 'forgive us our debts/sins as we forgive our debtors/those who offend us...' I was told to stop because that was the judgment. I began to wonder what all this was supposed to mean.

Generally, I was told that Jesus' blood has washed away our sins but what goes on in people's heart at any particular time is paramount. It was immediately after that statement that the angel conversing with me clapped his hands three times and something like a weighing scale landed on a table in our front. My sins were put on one side of the scale, and the measure of forgiveness I gave to people was put on the other side of the scale. All this while I thought I was doing well, but what surprised me was that, the total measure of forgiveness I gave to people in life was a meagre 1%. Immediately I was told, "You don't forgive people," then I heard, depart! Suddenly a door opened swiftly and I saw myself walking through a dark corridor, people can only turn left. The walkway had a very strong concrete wall for that reason, no one can escape. There were lots of people walking through this pathway and shortly there in the front was a rusted iron gate, neither grey nor black which read, this is the Gate of Hell.

At the point which appeared like the Reception Desk of the Gate of Hell, was this creature with an image like a human, always chewing something like a chewing stick (most Nigerians will understand), pacing up and down and would spit on those passing by followed by a hiss before they enter Hell. As I looked, there was a line drawn on the floor which once people go past it, a heavy load drops from something like the ceiling and that was what they would carry on their head forever. I was shocked to see from where I was standing, one of our Church members who died six years ago as at the time of this encounter. Let us call her Jumbo. To the best of my knowledge, I would say Sister Jumbo was a true Christian, a wonderful woman and the entire Church believed she was in heaven. Alas! She was in hell, the only reason she was condemned to hell was because of anger. I was told my apartment was next to Jumbo's apartment, and it wasn't as spacious as that of Jumbo. I argued with the creature in-charge at the Reception Desk about how Jumbo was full of many good works and the numerous support she gave to our local Church at different times but to no avail. Each time I mentioned one good thing or the other about Jumbo, a book would open from the Cabinet Jumbo was carrying on her head, and it would be confirmed and the 'receptionist' would hiss and throw the book back, and that was how Jumbo remained there.

Somehow, the attention shifted to me and I asked the 'receptionist,' what was the offence that brought me here? Then I was told, "You don't forgive, you pretend." All of a sudden, I began to remember all those occasions that I refused to forgive people, and the most recent incident was mentioned to me. Also, I was told about all the good works that I had done in the past were like filthy rags and I was directed to read, Isaiah 64:6. I was told, 'sin is sin,' the one who stole is as guilty as the one who killed his or her fellow. At this point I lifted my left leg to go through the door still protesting about Jumbo then I heard my husband's voice and I felt like, two of us will challenge this man, (the receptionist), and get Jumbo out of here. But something unusual happened. All of a sudden I heard my husband singing this song,

The resurrection power come and do miracles in my life,

Today, today come and do miracles in my life...

The above song made me to turn around full circle and saw Jesus sitting majestically on His throne, to say it was majestic is an understatement, till today it is indescribable to me. At the time, I saw what looked like seven stars on His golden chair and the crown on His head was magnificently glorious. Then I heard Mama Don (a member of our Church who died some years ago), as I said earlier, still pleading with Jesus on her knees to forgive me. I didn't feel convicted in my heart until now, suddenly I started to feel remorseful. Again Mama Don said to Jesus, "Please send her back because of thy song, that is, the little baby that I gave birth to through Caesarean Section. It looked like to me, Jesus was unwilling initially to forgive me, but in a twinkle of an eye He had changed and now wearing the crown of thorns, and I saw His beaten and battered body that was bleeding profusely.

As I watched what would happen, Jesus said to me, "How long will you continue to nail me to the Cross?" Then I saw all the marks where Jesus was nailed to the Cross. He was still bleeding from His head to the rest of His body. The great moment came when He touched the bleeding blood on His body and started to rub it on me. He began from my head to my toes. But as soon as He rubbed His blood on my two feet, I saw my body bounced on the hospital bed and I heard, Oh God, she's back, we've got a pulse." The timing was divinely precise because it coincided with the time the hospital staff were carrying out their resuscitation procedure on me. Thanks be to God for the grace and mercy shown to me especially for sending me back. I spent three days at the hospital after the encounter and I was discharged. I give all the glory to God for the second chance. (Testimony ends).

Anger can lead to so many dangers, can any person in their right sense allow it to send them to hell? It is so sad but true that Jumbo is spending her eternity in hell now, (Jumbo is the pseudonym for the Church sister who died around 2013). What are you waiting for? And what should prevent you from forgiving that person and forget about the matter? Why don't you leave it for God to handle? David listened to Abigail and it wasn't long, precisely in ten days and God dealt with Nabal for him, 1 Samuel 25:37–38.

> 37 So it was, in the morning, when the wine had gone from Nabal, and his wife had told him these things, that his heart died within him, and he became like a stone. 38 Then it happened, after about ten days, that the LORD struck Nabal, and he died. 1 Samuel 25:37–38.

Typically, there is so much to lose if anyone fails to forgive the other person, do not delay. Failure to forgive people who have offended you should not make you to lose your precious soul to hell. Please forgive completely like David in the above scripture and forget about those issues so that they won't cost you your eternity in hell. Lastly, it is important to realise that God's grace was extended to some individuals when they were unforgiving, whereas, others never received grace like Pastor Mrs Adejoke Oloko. She has been granted a second chance and she now uses every opportunity available to her to evangelise Jesus Christ. You can watch the YouTube version on the web address provided below.[48]

---

[48] https://youtu.be/IpMPOeEU1wk. Cited on 19/05/2022

SPIRITUAL CHECK-UP

Forgiveness can allow people to enter a new world that is hurt-free and enjoy positive consequences, don't delay.

Pray, meditate and ask God to show you your spiritual condition so that you can be set free, John 8:36.

Therefore if the Son makes you free, you shall be free indeed. John 8:36.

....
....
....
....
....
....
....
....
....
....
....
....
....
....

APPENDIX 1

SAMPLE QUESTIONS

1. I can forgive but I can't forget, what is wrong in that?

2. Someone wronged me and I have stopped talking to the person because I wanted my space. Is that lack of forgiveness?

3. This person did something really bad to me, although she has apologised after some time. I have forgiven her but I cannot trust the person again. Is that lack of forgiveness?

4. This person offended me, apologised to me and I said okay, but deep in my heart I have resolved to deal with him/her in a certain way. Please read Chapter 10 of this book.

It is important for every Christian believer to take responsibility for all their actions while alive and correct themselves before too late, and always remember that the Bible commands us to forgive one another, Colossians 3:13.

> Bearing with one another, and forgiving one another, if anyone has a complaint against another; even as Christ forgave you, so you also must do. Colossians 3:13.

APPENDIX 2

HELPFUL RESOURCES

Crisis and emotional support for any person affected by mental health:

Samaritans

Telephone - 116 123, 24-hours a day, 7 days a week

Website: www.samaritans.org

SaneLine

Telephone - 0300 304 7000, 7 days a week

Website: http://www.sane.org.uk/what_we_do/support/helpline

Mind Infoline

Provides information on types of mental health issues, where to get help, medication and alternative treatment and advocacy

Telephone - 0300 123 3393

Text: 86463

Self-help Books

10 Keys to Happier Living – A Practical Handbook, London, Headline Publishing Group: 2016

Gilbert, P., *The Compassionate Mind*, Constable: 2000

Greenberger, D. & Padesky, C.A., *Mind Over Mood: Change How You Feel by Changing How You Think*, Guildford Press: 2015

Harold S.K., *When Bad Things Happen to Good People*, Pan Books: 1981

Smedes, L.B., *Forgive and Forget - Healing The Hurts We Don't Deserve*, HarperCollins Publishers: 1996

BIBLIOGRAPHY

Ajibolorunrin, I.O., *The Nature of Grace – From the Perspective of Genesis 6:8,* London: Canada Christian College and School of Graduate Theological Studies, 2020

Ajibolorunrin, I.O., *The Significance of the Church's Mission and Ministry,* (An Extract from Master's Degree Material), London: Canada Christian College and School of Graduate Theological Studies, May 2019

Harrison, E.F., *The Wycliffe Bible Commentary,* (Chicago: Moody Press, 1962)

Jeffress, J., *When Forgiveness Doesn't Make Sense,* (Colorado Springs, Colorado: Waterbrook Press, 2000)

Keeley, R., (Organising Editor), *An Introduction to Christian Faith,* (Oxford: Lynx Communications, 1992)

Ladd, G.E., *Contribution on The Book of Acts,* in Everett F. Harrison, ed., The Wycliffe Bible Commentary, (Chicago: Moody Press: 1962)

Long, A., *Listening,* (London, Daybreak, Darton, Longman, and Todd, Ltd, 1990)

MacDonald, W., (Art Farstad, ed.), *Believer's Bible Commentary,* (London: Thomas Nelson Publishers, 1989)

Ryan, C.L., *European Theological Seminar – Connecting Ministry with Holy Scripture,* (Birmingham: Majesty Print: 2001)

Ryan, C.L., *Introduction to Apologetics and Evangelism,* (Compilation)

Sinclair, J.M., *Collins Dictionary & Thesaurus,* (Glasgow, Gt Britain: HarperCollins Publishers, 2000)

Smedes, B.L., *Forgive and Forget – Healing the Hurts We Don't Deserve,* (New York: HarperCollins Publishers, 1996)

Thiessen, H.C., *Lectures in Systematic Theology,* (Cambridge: William B. Eerdmans Publishing Company, 2006)

Tidball, D.J., *Skillful Shepherd – Explorations in Pastoral Theology,* (Leicester: Inter-Varsity Press, 1997)

Williams, D., (Ed.), *New Concise Bible Dictionary,* (Leicester: England, Inter-Varsity Press, 1989)

Devotional

Ademuyiwa, J., *Dose of Heaven Daily Devotional*, London, In His Presence Christ Tabernacle, 20 March 2020, Edition

Ademuyiwa, J., *Dose of Heaven Daily Devotional*, London, In His Presence Christ Tabernacle, 20 July 2020, Edition

Bibles

Amplified Bible (AMP)

Copyright © 2015 by The Lockman Foundation, La Habra, CA 90631. All rights reserved.

The Living Bible

Life Application Bible, Verses marked TLB are taken from The Living Bible copyright © 1971. Used by permission of Tyndale House Publishers, Inc., Wheaton, Illinois 60189. All rights reserved.

New King James Version

Scripture taken from the New King James Version®. Copyright © 1982 by Thomas Nelson. Used by permission. All rights reserved.

Websites

https://www.biblegateway.com

https://youtu.be/IpMPOeEU1wk Cited on 19/05/2022

FaithGateway Today, <newsletter@e.faithgateway.com> *I can heal. I can forgive. I can trust God..* — Lysa TerKeurst, *Forgiving What You Can't Forget.*

Matthew Henry's Commentary - Online, p. 2, (https://www.biblegateway.com)

www.ingramcontent.com/pod-product-compliance
Lightning Source LLC
LaVergne TN
LVHW011913080426
835508LV00007BA/510